R. Dawson

Notes on the High School Reader

R. Dawson

Notes on the High School Reader

ISBN/EAN: 9783337158620

Printed in Europe, USA, Canada, Australia, Japan

Cover: Foto ©Paul-Georg Meister /pixelio.de

More available books at **www.hansebooks.com**

NOTES

ON THE

HIGH SCHOOL READER.

THIRD CLASS LITERATURE FOR 1886-7.

BY

R. DAWSON, B.A., T.C.D.

HEAD MASTER WESTON HIGH SCHOOL,

Toronto:
ROSE PUBLISHING COMPANY,
1887.

PREFACE.

The Notes herewith presented are the prelude and harbingers to a complete annotation of the High School Reader; and they are issued in this separate form at the request of many of the teachers in our Public Schools, High Schools, and Collegiate Institutes, in order that their pupils might have in their hands, at as early a date as possible, the portion of the complete work bearing directly on the subjects prescribed for the next ensuing Examination of Candidates for Teachers' Certificates.

As to the general plan followed in these notes, it may be stated briefly:

(1) An effort has been made to present such Biographical Sketches, at least of the more important authors, as would inspire the student with a living interest in the subject of the sketch. Nothing is related of any author except such incidents as seemed to bear directly either on the formation of his character, or of his style ; and wherever it seemed advisable to guide the student to a fair estimate of his author, such clues have been thrown out as appeared most likely to answer the purpose.

(2) The well-read teacher will no doubt detect many points in which the critical estimate here given differs, and in some cases widely, from the average estimate of the professional critics—e.g. as to the literary value of the laureate odes of Tennyson—but if these divergences from the too well beaten path serve no other purpose, they may at least help the pupils to understand that the chains of mere authority may be too galling, and that in literary criticism, as in all other branches of human learning, the grand desideratum is that each should learn to think for himself, and be able to give a reason for the faith that is in him.

(3) If the pupil has been very frequently warned against the sceptical tendency of much of our verses of to-day, it is not only because it seemed well to guard thoughtless readers against the subtlety of agnostic poison, but because, from a purely literary view, it seemed that the baleful influence of the new No-creed is likely to be as fatal to poetry as to morals and religion.

(4) It ought not to be necessary to offer any apologies for the introduction of so much Etymological matter into the notes. Surely the time has come when we ought to make an effort to lift our more advanced pupils, and especially those who are about to become teachers of others, out of the worn rut of mere Latin and Greek roots, and to let them see that their language, the noblest and most useful that has yet been developed among men, belongs to an immense family of languages, of which Latin and Greek are but humble members, It will be noticed that wherever the Etymology clearly pointed to an Anglo-Saxon root, this has been given to the exclusion frequently of the other forms in which the same root appears in cognate dialects ; this has been done partly to avoid unnecessary detail, partly in order not to impose too severe a task on the memory of the student. For the same reason the annotator has, except in a very few instances, shunned the temptation, to which his early studies exposed him, of referring words in our language back to the Sanscrit roots in which most words in the Aryan languages occur in their most ancient, and therefore purest forms.

In conclusion, any suggestions for the improvement of these notes will be thankfully received by the publishers and the author.

R. DAWSON.

High School,
    Weston, Jan., 1887.

NOTES

ON

THE HIGH SCHOOL READER.

THIRD CLASS LITERATURE FOR 1886-7.

JOSEPH ADDISON.—1672–1719.

THE GOLDEN SCALES.—Extract XV., page 88.

Biographical Sketch.—Joseph Addison, the eldest son of Lancelot Addison, dean of Lichfield, was born at the rectory of Milston, Wiltshire, May 1st, 1672. He received his early education mainly at the Charterhouse, where he had for schoolfellow and friend a lad of Irish parentage, Dick Steele, with whom he was subsequently associated in the production of the *Tatler* and the *Spectator*. At the age of 15 he entered the University of Oxford, matriculating at Queen's College but removing two years later to Magdalen College, which had awarded him a scholarship for excellence in Latin verse composition. At the University he formed a close friendship with his fellow-student, Sacheverell, and this friendship appears to have continued unbroken in spite of the differences of political opinion that existed between them from the first.

Addison was intended for the Church, and being naturally of a serious and sedate disposition he became an ardent student and admirer of Milton and the other Puritan writers of the preceding generation, from whom he imbibed a fondness for religious reflection, a love of Biblical research, and a mild passion for the abstract principles advocated by the Whig leaders of the period. Oxford was at that time the educational stronghold of Toryism, and the appearance there of a promising young Whig was sufficiently phenomenal to attract the serious attention of the leaders of the party. Halifax and Somers warmly encouraged the literary aspirations of the young Oxonian, and he consequently abandoned his intention of entering the Church, though he never gave up his early convictions on the side of true religion, nor the habit of unconscious sermonizing into which he had been beguiled by his early training.

In 1693 he took his M.A. degree, and in this year his apprenticeship to a literary career may be said to have fairly begun. His political friends could not yet see their way to do much more than encourage him by promises, and for the next few years he earned a somewhat precarious subsistence and a steadily growing reputation by his pen. A poem addressed to the veteran Dryden, and incorporated by him in his Miscellanies, some excellent translations and imitations of the classics, laudatory verses on contemporary great men, a turgid poem, " *To the King*," celebrating the continental wars of William III., with the taking of Namur, and other pieces of a like kind at length convinced Somers that his party and the nation at large would profit by affording the young poet the means of more extended observation and study of mankind. Accordingly, in 1699, he received a pension of £300 a year, to enable him "to travel and qualify himself to serve His Majesty." The next three or four years were spent on the Continent, where he visited France, Italy, Switzerland, Germany, and Holland. During his travels he was unconsciously perfecting his literary style by jotting down descriptions and observations in the easy and familiar language of ordinary correspondence. His *Letter from Italy* is by far the best of his more pretentious poems, though it can hardly be said to have survived as a part of the permanent literature of the language.

The death of William and downfall of the Whig administration put an end to his travels, and in 1703 he returned to England. where he was shortly afterwards admitted to the Kitcat Club,* the rendezvous and rallying point of the Whig gentry.

In 1704 Godolphin, on the recommendation of Halifax, employed him to write *The Campaign*, celebrating the victory of Blenheim, and rewarded him for his services by appointing him to succeed the celebrated Locke as Commissioner of Appeals in Excise. "The Campaign" was received with the utmost enthusiasm, due rather to the patriotism of the readers than to the poetic merit of the composition. One merit, however, it does possess; it is the first poem of the kind in which the old machinery of gods and demigods is discarded, and the actors are presented to us as living, rational human beings.

Henceforward the career of Addison was a continual triumph in public, though marred by the domestic unhappiness that has rendered wretched the lives of so many of our best and purest masters of English literature. Transferred from his garret in the Haymarket by the success of *The Campain*, his advancement was phenomenally rapid; he speedily became Under Secretary of State,

---

* So ramed from its meeting at the house of one Christopher, or Kit, Cat.

(1706); accompanied Halifax (1707), as Secretary, in his mission to the Court of the Elector of Hanover; entered parliament (1708) for the old pocket-borough of Lostwithiel; went to Ireland as Secretary under the *régime* of Lord Wharton (1709); and in 1710 was returned for Malmesbury, which he represented (being six times re-elected) till his death.

The virtual failure of the Government in the prosecution of his friend Sacheverell led to the downfall of the Whig ministry in 1710, and gave Addison the opportunity of enriching our literature with a series of graceful, polished, and refined essays, hailed in his own day with an eager enthusiasm such as has never been extended to similar productions, read and studied with a keen delight by every reader since their first appearance, and destined to maintain their place as models of style so long as English literature and the English language shall endure.

During Addison's absence in Ireland his old schoolfellow, Steele, had originated the periodical miscellany, by the production of the *Tatler*, "a tri-weekly sheet, giving the latest items of news, and following them up with a tale or essay." Addison recognized the authorship at once, and aided the enterprise almost from the beginning, in April, 1709, till the close of the series in January, 1711. The *Tatler* was followed by the daily *Spectator*, a non-political journal, to the pages of which Addison, Steele, Pope, and others contributed some of the most delightful papers to be found in the ephemeral literature of any country or of any age. Addison, indeed, regarded his contributions as by no means ephemeral. In the tenth number he tells us, with a spice of the pardonable egotism from which he was by no means free, that as Socrates had "brought philosophy down from heaven to inhabit among men;—I should be ambitious to have it said of me that I have brought philosophy out of closets and libraries, schools and colleges, to dwell in clubs and assemblies, at tea-tables and in coffee-houses." A certain kind of philosophy he undoubtedly did bring before the reading public of his day—the philosophy of patience, resignation, and sound common sense,—but the reader will search the pages of the *Spectator* in vain for anything at all approaching to the depth of philosophical insight displayed by John Locke, his predecessor in the Commissionership of Excise, or even by Pope, his co-laborer in the pages of the *Spectator*. Addison was by no means a profound thinker ; nor was profound thought needed for the production of such essays, letters, witticisms, and criticisms as those with which he delighted his contemporaries. Men were weary of the long political struggle that had been strangling the energies of the nation, and they gladly welcomed the light grace and tender humor of the miscellaneous papers, in which the lessons of tolerance, kindness, and Christian charity were taught so wisely and so well.

Contributions to the pages of the *Guardian*, the *Freeholder*, and the *Whig Examiner*, together with *The Late Trial and Conviction of Count Tariff*,—an attack on the Tories for their share in the Treaty of Utrecht, written in reply to Arbuthnot's satirical *History of John Bull*—complete the series of Addison's political writings ; but none of these productions, though successful enough at the time, can be said to have survived, nor is any of them marked by that well-bred, gentlemanly grace that so distinctly marks his papers in the *Spectator*.

In 1713, Addison's tragedy, *Cato*, was produced, and was received with thunders of applause,—the Whigs extolling it as a plea for constitutional liberty, and the Tories supporting it to show their abhorrence of tyranny, and pretending to recognize the great Whig general, Marlborough, in the character of Julius Cæsar.

The sudden death of Queen Anne brought the Whigs and Addison once more into power, and he became Secretary to the Provisional Government of the Lords Justices, was appointed one of the Lords of the Board of Trade, and subsequently Secretary of State. In 1716 he married the Countess dowager of Warwick, with whom he is said to have lived unhappily ; and in 1719, after an inglorious quarrel with his old friend Steele, the greatest master of English prose that the century had produced, died the peaceful death of a Christian, in presence, it is said, of his step-son, the young Earl of Warwick, whom he had summoned to his bed-side to see how a Christian could die.

The prose style of Addison is especially remarkable for its freedom from mannerism of any kind, and perhaps the best service he has rendered to literature is the useful lesson he has taught—that the ordinary language of everyday life is eminently suited to literary requirements, and that the easy colloquial grace of a well-bred gentleman is not at all inconsistent with a style of noble and dignified eloquence. Other services, too, he has rendered to literature ;—he was the first to bring Milton's writings to the notice of the reading world ; he was the first to discard the absurd machinery of mythology from modern poetry ; he was among the first to appeal to the verdict of the public instead of relying merely on the patronage of some great man for the success of his literary productions ; and, finally, he and his friend Steele have left us a portrait-gallery of characters from which the Sternes, Dickenses, Thackerays and others have been able to draw their most life-like figures without in the slightest degree despoiling the original canvas.

THE GOLDEN SCALES.

The extract is from the *Spectator* of August 21, 1712, and is a very fair specimen of Addison's average style in his didactic essays. The object of the paper is to inculcate the sound practical lesson "not to despise or value any things for their appearances, but— according to their real and intrinsic value ;" and the essayist very gracefully leads up to this object by an appropriate introduction recounting the manner in which the Supreme Being estimates the affairs of earth according to ancient mythology and the records of inspired writ.

To the instances given in the text the author might have added the description given by Arctinus of Miletus, of the weighing by Apollo and Mercury of the fates of Achilles and Memnon. It corresponds with Milton's account more closely than either of those given in the text, the opponents being represented in the scales by their respective genii, or familiar guardian spirits.

Homer's balance—The allusion here is to the passage in the 17th Book of the Iliad, in which Zeus (Jupiter) is represented as balancing the fates of Hector and Achilles, the bravest chiefs, respectively, of the Trojans and Greeks. The scale of Hector is represented by Homer as descending, thus foreshadowing his descent to the tomb. In an earlier book, the 8th, the fates of Greece and Troy in an impending struggle are weighed, but on that occasion, inasmuch as Achilles had retired from active participation in the war, the scale of Greece is in like manner made to descend in presage of their defeat. Virgil's description is a paraphrase of Homer's, and accordingly the fatal lot is shown by the descent of the scale. Milton's description depicts the would-be combatants as represented in the scales, and Satan is shown "how light, how weak," &c.

Homer's birthplace is uncertain ; the following elegiac couplet names the more important of the many places that claimed the honor :—

> Smyrna, Chios, Colophon, Salamis, Rhodus, Argos, Athenæ,
> Orbis de patriâ certat, Homere, tuâ.

The universal belief of antiquity was that he was blind, but beyond this fact, if fact it be, we know nothing more than that he composed, but did not write, his two immortal poems about the eighth century, B. C. The *Iliad* celebrates the "wrath of Achilles" against Agamemnon, the captain-general of the Greeks, with its causes, consequences, and ultimate appeasement. In the *Odyssey* are celebrated the wanderings of Ulysses (Odysseus) on his return voyage from the siege of Troy.

Hector—son of Priam, king of Troy, and Hecuba, was the bravest of all the Trojan heroes. His death at the hands of Achilles, and the lamentations at his burial form some of the most striking and pathetic episodes of the Iliad.

Achilles—son of Peleus, king of Phthia, and the sea-nymph Thetis, was the representative hero of the Greeks during the closing scenes of the Trojan war. Mythology represents in several forms the desire of his mother that he should be long-lived. She is represented as trying to render him invulnerable by placing him in boiling water, according to one account, or in fire, as another version gives it, and anointing his body with ambrosia ; while a later and more popular form of the myth describes his being dipped in the river Styx and thus rendered invulnerable except in the heel, by which his mother had held him during his immersion. In the Iliad he appears as the leader of the Hellenes, a name then applied only to the tribe commanded by him, but subsequently extended so as to embrace all of Greek extraction wherever situated.

Turnus—prince of the Rutuli, was a rival of Æneas for the hand of Lavinia, and was slain by him in single combat.

Æneas—Next to Hector the prize of valor amongst the Trojans must be awarded to Æneas. Virgil, in the Æneid, describes his wanderings and vicissitudes from the time of his escape from Troy till his landing in Italy, where he married Lavinia, daughter of king Latinus, and became the father of Æneas Silvius, the founder of the Silvian dynasty at Alba Longa and progenitor of Romulus, the equally mythical founder and first king of Rome.

Virgil—Publius Virgilius Maro was born at Andes, a small village near Mantua, 70 B.C. The loss of his small patrimony drove him to Rome where he acquired the friendship of Augustus and his prime minister Mæcenas, as well as that of the poet Horace and other celebrated writers of the period. His immortal epic, the *Æneid*, has justly placed him in the foremost rank of epic poets, where he stands side by side in the temple of fame with Homer and our own Milton.

Milton—1608–1674—John Milton was the son of a London scrivener, by whom he was destined for the Church, but refusing to take the necessary oaths, he, instead, devoted himself to literature and the cause of civil and religious liberty. Educated at Christ College, Cambridge, he afterwards travelled on the Continent, where he formed the acquaintance of several distinguished writers and philosophers, including Galileo, then suffering an unwilling martyrdom at the hands of the Inquisition. His connection with the Puritan party subjected him to the resentment of Charles II. on his Restoration, and the days of the poet were spent in concealment and in sorrow till the Act of Oblivion relieved him from his well-grounded fears for his personal safety. His eyesight had been sacrificed in unremitting labors on behalf of the Protector and the Regicides, whom he defended against the accusations of Salmasius in a controversy memorable for its virulence; and for the last twenty years of his life his lot was embittered by physical blindness added to poverty, neglect, and regret for the apparent failure of the cause of liberty to which he had devoted his life.

Paradise Lost is in some respects—as, for instance, in choice of subject,—the grandest epic that the world has yet seen; but it remained comparatively unknown to the public of England till the criticisms of Addison, in the *Spectator*, directed general attention to its existence. It was finished in 1655, the year after the poet had become blind, and the manuscript was sold for the paltry sum of five guineas, with the stipulation that five guineas more should be paid on the sale of thirteen hundred copies. Milton died in 1674, Addison being then just two and a half years old.

The great king of Babylon—Belshazzar, associated with his father Nabonnedus (Labynetus) as joint ruler of Babylon, *see Daniel* v. 1–30. The joint sovereignty of Labynetus and his son accounts for the peculiar form of the reward conferred on Daniel for his interpretation of the mystic writing—*See* Rawlinson, as quoted in *Testimony of the Ages*.

Other places of the holy writings—in *Job*, the *Psalms*, and the *Proverbs*. The idea of weighing the fates of mortals was a very common one in the ancient world, and is portrayed on many of the Egyptian papyri and monuments.

Foregoing instances, = preceding, forementioned, examples. The word *forego*, as used here (A.S. *fore* = in front, and *gán* = to go) is not to be confounded with the other verb *forego* = to give up, to relinquish, which should be spelt *forgo* (A.S. *for*, a privative prefix, and *gán* = to go) as in *forbid*, *forget*, &c.

Addressing themselves, = directing, getting ready—(L. *ad*, and *directus*, p. p. of *dirigo*, the low Latin form of which is *drictus*).

Betwixt Astræa and the Scorpion sign—The constellation Libra (the Scales) is one of the signs of the Zodiac, between Virgo (the Virgin) and the Scorpion. Lucan and Virgil (Ecl. 4–6) identify Astræa with the constellation Virgo; and Ovid represents her (Astræa) as the goddess of Justice, daughter of Jupiter and Themis. The signs of the Zodiac in order may be easily remembered from the following (almost) doggerel stanza :—

> The Ram, the Bull, the heavenly Twins,
> Then next the Crab the Lion shines,
> The Virgin and the Scales ;

The Scorpion, Archer, and He-Goat,
The man that holds the Watering-pot,
And Fish with glittering scales.

Pendulous—derived directly from the Latin *pendulus* = hanging, cf. *pendere* = to hang.

Balanced—Fr. *balance*, Lat. *bilanx*, th. *bis* = twice, i.e. double and *lanx* = dish, or hollow vessel, cf. *lacus*, Eng. *lake*.

Ponders—lit. weighs, then metaphorically, weighs in mind. The literal meaning of the word in this passage is much more poetical than its ordinary metaphorical sense.

Sequel (*sequela*, *sequor* = to follow) = that which shows the consequence, or result. Note the peculiar use of *each*.

Kick'd the beam—swung in against and struck, kicked, the beam, or bar, of the scales, thereby showing its extreme lightness. *Kick*, th. Welsh *cicio*, to strike with the *cic*, or foot.

Fiend, Satan—Both words mean an enemy, a hater. *Fiend*, p. p. of A. S. *fion* = to hate, as *friend* is the p. p. of *fri* = to love—cf, Freya, the Venus, goddess of love, of the Teutons. *Satan* is from the Hebrew *Sátan* = to persecute.

Since thine, &c.—Obviously *strength*, not *arms*. Supply the ellipses in the whole passage from Milton. Parse *mine—nor more*.

You—common enough in the days of Shakspeare and of Milton, now only used as a provincial colloquialism. Same root as yea, yes, yet, ye, you.

Amusing thoughts—Thomson uses the word *amusive;* is there any difference between the words? *Thought*, A. S. *thencan* = to think.

Methought, = it seemed to me. A. S. *thincan* = to seem. The word is only used in a quasi-impersonal way, having always a noun sentence for its subject; *me* being an indirect dative object.

Replaced = placed again. What is its present meaning?

Chain in the same metal—Translate into modern English.

Essay, cf. *assay*.—The word is derived from the Latin *exagium*, Gr. ἐξάγιον, and originally meant a *weighing*, so that it is used here in its strictly literal sense. Give the present meaning of the word. How does it differ from *assay*, its original form ?

Note the delicate humor and sound common sense of the remainder of the extract ; and, having carefully read it, reproduce it in your own words. Excellent themes for composition may be found in a comparison of the real and apparent values of the several qualities and endowments mentioned. Observe the preponderating weight of Eternity ; the surprising effect of vanity ; the value of adversity ; the equality of avarice and poverty, of riches and con-

tent ; the enhanced value of one good quality by having another
added to it ; and the graceful play of the serio-comic paragraph
immediately preceding the solemn gravity of the brief concluding
reflection.

Give the exact meanings of the words used to indicate the
several qualities, good or bad, mentioned in the extract.

" In the dialect of men, Calamities. In the language of the gods, Blessings "—Compare with the sentiment here expressed Shakspeare's—

> " Sweet are the uses of Adversity ;"

and Longfellow's beautiful lines in *Resignation :*—

> " Let us be patient ; what we call Afflictions
> Not from the ground arise ;
> And oftentimes celestial Benedictions
> Assume this dark disguise."

Natural parts—i.e., cleverness, intellect—often used in this
sense by writers of Addison's time.

Phenomenon—Gr. φαίνομαι, first = *an appearance,* and
by an easy addition, *an unusual appearance.*

Fails of dashing—would now be regarded as an Archaism.
What is the present form? **Impertinence**—that which does
not belong to (*in,* not, and *pertinens,* belonging to) the matter.
Distinguish *impertinence, impudence, insolence.*

The first trial—What trial ? Refer to the passage in the
extract.

Throwing into one scale—and in the other—" Bonus
dormitat Homerus." Even Addison sometimes nods. See also
the opening sentence of the extract, and re-write both paragraphs.

A neutral paper—The *Spectator* was the first successful
non-political paper published in England.

OLIVER GOLDSMITH.—1728-1774.

From THE VICAR OF WAKEFIELD.—Extract XXII., page 127.

Biographical Sketch—The most entertaining biography in the English language is Boswell's *Life of Samuel Johnson*, and by far the most entertaining figure in that pre-Raphaelite portrait gallery is the figure of Oliver Goldsmith.. In the garrulous pages that record the sayings and doings of the members of "The Club,"—the ponderous judgments of the burly central figure, and the more or less weighty but always brilliant utterances of the rest, --the reader meets the uncouth form, the ugly face, and the blundering speeches of Goldsmith, with a relief hardly to be accounted for by our knowledge that this gay, frivolous, fantastic chatterbox is nevertheless one of the greatest writers in the English language.

Born at Pallas, in the Co. Longford, Ireland, in 1728, where his father, the Rev. Charles Goldsmith, eked out the scanty living derived from an ill-paid curacy, by farming and economy, the boy who was destined to make English literature known to the scholars of Europe, spent his earliest years in the most abject poverty. But while Oliver was yet a child his father was promoted to the parish of Lissoy, in the county of Westmeath ; and here the boy was taught the alphabet by a kind servant girl, whose patient perseverance overcame his impenetrable stupidity. In his seventh year he was sent to a village school, kept by an old soldier, Thomas Byrne, from whom he acquired a love for songs, stories, and romances, and whom he has depicted with a loving hand in the *Deserted Village.*

At the age of seventeen he entered Trinity College, Dublin, as a sizar, a position which at that time subjected the holder to humiliations unendurable by a sensitive spirit like Goldsmith's ; and it is hardly to be wondered that he reaped little advantage from his University career, beyond the more extended knowledge of human nature derived from his association with the more turbulent spirits of the college and the vagrant ballad singers of the city.

Having taken his degree he returned to his now widowed mother, and spent the next couple of years in the hopeless task of looking out for a profession. Presenting himself for ordination in a scarlet hunting dress, borrowed for the occasion, he was very properly and promptly ejected from the Episcopal mansion. An attempt at teaching was hardly more successful. He went to Cork with the intention of emigrating to America, but missed his ship and returned home after spending the money that had been raised to pay his passage. A generous kinsman lent him fifty pounds to begin the study of the law, but the allurements of a Dublin gaming house proved too strong for his weak resolution and his money went even more quickly than on the previous escapade. He was next sent to Edinburgh, and subsequently to the University of Leyden, to study medicine ; but systematic study was an impossibility to the graceless Oliver, and he failed to obtain a medical diploma at either institution.

Leaving Leyden he began to make the grand tour of the continent, as Addison had done before him. Unlike Addison, however, the poor young Irishman had no Government pension to render his path easy ; and he was obliged to earn the scanty subsistence that sufficed him by playing on his flute for the amusement of the peasants, and occasionally by procuring a meal and a night's lodging at a convent as a reward for his ingenuity in debating. He thus rambled on foot through Flanders, France, Switzerland, and part of Italy ; and in this way he acquired the materials afterwards turned to such a good account in *The Traveller*, and in *The Vicar of Wakefield.*

In 1756 he landed at Dover, and for the next few years he led such a life of misery as has fallen to the lot of comparatively few of even the most suffering sons of genius. He became an actor in a third-rate company of strolling players, an usher in a cheap school, an apothecary's assistant, a beggar, even, herding with vagrant outcasts in the purlieus of London. At last he settled down to the miserable work of an ill-paid, much-abused literary hack ; and to this worst of trades—worse then than it is now—the brilliant outcast devoted several of the best years of his life, till his genius, having by long practice acquired the art of easy expression, displayed itself in the production of works that have rendered the name of Goldsmith renowned wherever the English tongue is spoken.

In 1763 he was admitted to the celebrated club of which Johnson, Garrick, Burke, Reynolds, Beauclerk, and Boswell were the leading members. In 1764, the publication of *The Traveller*, the first work to which he had put his name, at once raised him to the rank of a classic, and paved the way for the success of *The Vicar of Wakefield*, the manuscript of which had been sold for him in the same year by Dr. Johnson, to pay the arrears of his rent to his landlady, according to the well-known story. From this time forward his literary success was assured, the booksellers vieing with each other to secure the productions of his pen ; and he might have enjoyed a life of ease and affluence if he had been endowed in fact with even a modicum of the good sense so conspicuous in his pages. But good sense was almost the only good quality that he did not in some degree possess. He had been a wayward, generous spendthrift when a boy ; and a wayward, generous spendthrift he continued to the end.   For the last ten years of his life he was in receipt of a handsome income ; but reckless generosity, extravagance, and gambling kept him poor, and even involved him so heavily in debt that his health and spirits finally gave way under the strain, and in 1774 he died of a nervous fever.

His services to literature are many. He was the first to show how a school text-book should be written, and his abridgements of the *Histories of Greece, Rome*, and *England*, though faulty and inaccurate, are still models of what school histories might be.   His *Animated Nature*, bristling with absurdities, was yet the first book to make the study of nature interesting, and therefore popular.   His *Traveller* was one of the pioneers in the introduction of natural description into poetry ; and the good work was still further aided by the *Deserted Village*, full though the latter is of startling incongruities.   The *Good-Natured Man* was the first attempt in that style of easy and vivacious comedy that reached its climax in the hands of Sheridan ; and though received coldly on its first production at Covent Garden in 1768 it yet paved the way for the still more rollicking humor of *She Stoops to Conquer*, with which he fairly took the town by storm, five years later, and drove forever from the boards the sickly sentimentality of the Kelly & Cumberland school, which men had previously mistaken for the production of the comic muse.   He has proved, quite as conclusively as Addison, that wit and coarseness are by no means necessarily connected ; and, though writing in and for a coarse age, not one sentence or sentiment of indecency can be found in all his writings.   And finally, in the exquisite little gem, *Retaliation*, published shortly after his death, he has convinced us that satirical portraiture can be successfully done without ill-humor or ill-nature.

The Vicar of Wakefield will probably retain its popularity as long as the English language lasts—a popularity not at all due to any inherent excellence in the plot or interest in the story.   Goldsmith was singularly deficient in the art of constructing a well-arranged, coherent plot ; his Irish blood probably predisposed him to a love of the incongruous, and it is at least doubtful whether he was himself aware how absurdly inconsistent are many of his plots and incidents.   But his Irish blood counterbalanced the defect by endowing him with that *subjective* temperament so markedly characteristic of the Irish people ; and few prose writers have so uniformly identified themselves with the characters of their own creation.   In the vicar, as in the village preacher of the *Deserted Village*, we have a portrait, drawn by a loving hand, of an ideal pastor combining the good qualities of the author's father and elder brother; but the thoughts, feelings, and reflections of the venerable clergyman are those of Goldsmith himself, and it is this power of projecting himself into his characters that makes them so intensely real in spite of all their incongruous surroundings. The plot of the romance is of the most meagre kind, the incidents are improbable, and the whole story consists rather of a series of moral homilies than a well-connected narrative. Each chapter is in fact, and almost in form, an essay intended to inculcate some special truth. But though thus faulty in form, character, and kind, the surpassing genius of the author has made *The Vicar of Wakefield* the most charming prose idyll in the English, or, indeed, in any language. It arrested the attention of Goëthe, and other great continental critics, and thus made English literature known and respected as no other work of the period could have done. The delightful grace and simplicity of the language has such a charm that while reading it we never think of testing the merits of the production by applying to it any of the established canons of criticism. No author has been so uniformly successful in blinding the eyes of his readers to that perfection of art which is almost the "*ars celandi artem.*" Everyone thinks that he could, without effort, write exactly as Goldsmith did. Misled by the perfect simplicity and harmony of the style, we imagine that we, too, would have expressed the same thoughts in the same words ; but, in truth, there are few authors whose mannerisms cannot be imitated with greater ease and success than can his perfect naturalness, and it is only by close study we discover that what seemed at first the least artificial of compositions is in reality the very perfection of the most polished art. It would not, indeed, be difficult to point out whole pages in the works of Goldsmith in which not one word could be altered or displaced without marring the symmetry and rhythm of the passage.

SCENE FROM THE VICAR OF WAKEFIELD.

The extract requires very little in the way of annotation. Note the exquisite humor that prevails throughout—the complacent vanity of the good vicar's wife and children, and his fruitless struggles to overcome it—the mother's pride in Olivia's beauty, and the "cunning, which everybody saw through," whereby she tried to lure the landlord to a proposal of marriage—the strange combination of utterly incongruous characters depicted in the memorable painting—and finally the carrying out of the "resolution which had too much cunning to give entire satisfaction" to the simple-minded head of the family. It will be good practice in composition to reproduce some of the more striking passages in the style of the author.

Sophia's sensations—The family at Wakefield consisted of the vicar, his wife Deborah, and six children. The eldest, George, is away from home at the time mentioned in the extract ; Olivia, the second, is in love with their landlord, Thornhill, a profligate young rake with dishonorable intentions, who is, however, ultimately foiled in his purpose ; Sophia, the third in order, has been saved from drowning by Mr. Burchell, and therefore she naturally enough feels his absence, caused by a temporary estrangement, more than it is felt by the rest of the family ; Moses, the fourth child, is a good-natured, blundering greenhorn, not at all unlike what Goldsmith himself had been at the same age ; the two remaining children are bright little lads, the sons of their parents' old age, and the pets of their elder brothers and sisters.

Disappointed in procuring my daughters, &c.—daughter = "the milker," from an Aryan root *duh* (for *dhugh*) = to milk. Parse the word.

The town—i.e. London, commonly called "the town" by the writers of the period.

The play-houses=theatres. These favorite resorts of the "high wits" had to a considerable extent recovered from the immorality into which they had been plunged during the Restoration period.

Good things — witticisms. **Jest-books**—the name commonly given to collections of wit and humor. *Joe Miller's Jest-Book* is the most celebrated of them all.

Piquet—a fashionable game at cards ; perhaps a diminutive of *pique*, i.e. a small contest.

Ate short and crisp = were short and crisp in the eating. *Ate* is used here as an intransitive verb of incomplete predication, *short* and *crisp* being the subjective complements.

Gooseberry—commonly, but erroneously, derived from *gorse berry;* the word is a hybrid, made up of the Old French *groise* and the English *berry*, the original form being *groise berry*, or *grose berry.*

Squire—originally " the shield-bearer (*scutiger*) of a knight."

Extremely of a size = of exactly the same height. A writer of the present day would not employ such a phrase, but its meaning is clear enough.

To see which was tallest—Is the superlative form admissible ? Possibly the word is purposely put in the old lady's mouth, she not being expected to be as choice in her language as her learned husband.

Neighbor Flamborough's—a worthy parishioner of the vicar.

Limner—a painter, fr. Lat. *illuminare* by omission of the prefix.

No variety in life, no composition in the world—Note the change of phrase, and observe that *composition* is used here in its technical sense, to indicate the arrangement and grouping of the figures in a picture. Mark, also, how the affectation of artistic knowledge heightens the effect of the incongruities in their own "family piece." Specify in detail all the incongruities referred to.

To hit us = to suit us, to hit our fancy.

Venus—the Roman goddess of love, corresponding to the Aphrodite of the Greeks, would be the very last being likely to appreciate the vicar's defence of Whiston.

Stomacher—an ornamental covering for the breast.

Cupids—Originally there was only one Cupid, son of Venus, but later legends represented several. Cupid was generally represented as a chubby boy-god, winged, and armed with a bow, and a quiver full of love-darts.

The Whistonian controversy—The Rev. William Whiston, philosopher and mathematician, succeeded his friend Sir Isaac Newton as professor of Mathematics at Cambridge, but was subsequently deprived of his professorship on account of his embracing the heresy of the Arians, who deny that the Son is co-eternal and co-essential with the Father. One of Whiston's opinions was that it is not lawful for a Church of England clergyman to marry again on the death of his first wife, and the "books on the Whistonian controversy" consisted of the vicar's sermons in defence of Whiston's position on this point. The same doctrine is held by the clergy of the Greek Church.

As an Amazon—The Amazons were a mythical race of female warriors in Scythia, who were described as having cut off their right breasts in order to facilitate their use of the bow: whence their name was derived, Gr. $\dot{\alpha}$ = not, and $\mu\alpha\zeta\acute{o}s$ = the breast. Another version of the myth locates them on the banks of the river Thermodon in Asia Minor.

With an hat and white feather—*With* was frequently used as an equivalent for *wearing*—cf. "*with* my gown and band." The rule requiring *a* before a consonant was not always observed in the case of words beginning with *h* sounded; cf. p. 130, last line, "choice of *an* husband."

Alexander, the Great—son of Philip, king of Macedon, was born at Pella, 356, B.C.,—succeeded his father at the age of twenty—conquered nearly the whole of the then known world—

and died at Babylon of a fever, 323 B.C. He was buried at Alexandria in Egypt, which city he had built to commemorate the conquest of that country.

To be introduced into, &c.—How is *introduce* now used?

An unfortunate circumstance had not occurred = presented itself to our minds. How is the word now used?

Which now struck us with dismay—Is there anything singular in the position of this clause? · Dismay, fr. A.S. *magán* lit. deprival of strength.

Robinson Crusoe's Long Boat—Every boy, and for that matter, every girl, ought to read *Robinson Crusoe*; it is the first in time, and very many competent young critics have held it to be the first in merit, of English novels. The author, Daniel Defoe, was born in 1661, and was one of the most prolific writers of the age. In 1719 the old political partisan produced this, his best known work, and it has probably been the delight of a greater number of readers than has any single romance that has appeared since then. One of the most humorous passages in *The Vicar of Wakefield* describes Olivia as seriously preparing herself for the work of reforming her rakish lover by a careful study of the conversations between Crusoe and his Man Friday.

A Reel in a Bottle—Such ingenious toys were more appreciated in the last century than in this ; not only *reels*, but even miniature models of full-rigged ships were not uncommonly displayed in bottles—instances of perverted ingenuity, and useless waste of time and money, having their counterpart in the vicar's great historical family picture.

Once again = once more. *Once*, old genitive, of *one*, used adverbially. *Again* = a second time. Is it used here in its strict sense?

Discover the honor of Mr. Thornhill's addresses = ascertain whether his addresses were honorable. The exact literal meaning is to *uncover*, *i.e.*, detect the worth of Mr., &c.

To sound him—The metaphor is taken from measuring the depth of water with a plummet.—a *sound* being a narrow channel of no great depth. Cf. The Sound.

It was then resolved to terrify him—The writers of Goldsmith's time were not so particular as to the position of the adverb as we are now. Re-write the sentence. What is the distinction between *terrify* and *frighten?*

Observe well the consummate art with which the scheme is described—the pride, the anxiety, and the transparent cunning of the poor mother—the flippant callousness of the profligate Thornhill, and his ill-concealed contempt for the understanding of the woman whose daughter he is seeking to ruin. There is no apparent effort to enlist us on the side of virtue, but, though the rake succeeds in mystifying his interlocutor, the author takes care not to allow him to impose upon the reader ; he is made to betray himself for the base, vulgar, cowardly, ill-bred debauchee that he is at heart, and we are made to feel that, with all her weakness and folly, it is still poor Deborah Primrose that has succeeded in carrying away our sympathies and our wishes for her success.

Note the contrast between the pleasant homeliness of the mother's language, and the stilted bombast of the squire. She, good soul, speaks of " a proper husband," " a warm man, able to give her good bread," farmer Williams, "who wants a manager," etc., etc., while he rants about "accomplishments," and " angels," and " goddesses," in a way that must have convinced her of his insincerity had she not been so deeply interested in the success of her innocent device.

LORD BYRON—1788-1824.

Tɴᴇ Iꜱʟᴇꜱ ᴏꜰ Gʀᴇᴇᴄᴇ.—Extract XXXV., page 211.

Biographical Sketch.—George Noël Gordon Byron was born in Holles street, London, on the 22nd January, 1788 ; and from the first moments of his existence he was beset by influences which rendered him fiercely impatient of his surroundings, and thus fitted him to take his place as *the* poet of the revolution— the masterly leader of the revolt against the humdrum spirit of the eighteenth century. His father, Captain Byron, was a profligate scoundrel, who had squandered the fortune of his wife, Catherine Gordon, and had then shamelessly abandoned her and his unborn son. His grand-uncle, from whom he inherited the title and the encumbered estate of Newstead Abbey, having killed his kinsman, Mr. Chaworth, in a brawl, had, by his subsequent debaucheries, acquired the sobriquet of " wicked Lord Byron." His mother was a woman of a most violent and spasmodic temper, one day treating him with a passionate tenderness, and the next, hurling missiles at the "lame brat" for some childish exhibition of stubborn self-will. Their impoverished condition deprived them of the comforts and the outward respect which would have been theirs but for the selfish extravagance of the scoundrel who had deserted them ; and this, while it embittered the earliest years of the poet, made it almost impossible for him to entertain a high respect for the sanctity of such marriages of convenience as that of which he was the unhappy offspring.

Under such influences the child grew up, at Aberdeen, till the death of the "wicked Lord Byron," in 1798, raised him to the peerage, and added to the moodiness of his disposition by gratifying his boyish pride without affording him the means necessary for the becoming support of his position. Having acquired a large amount of general information from desultory reading, but very little accurate knowledge of the usual school-boy studies, he went to the great Public School at Harrow, in 1801, where he was distinguished for his omnivorous reading in literature and history, his ambition to excel in all the athletic sports of the school, and the passionate depth of his attachments and affection for his school-boy friends. Intensity of feeling characterized him from his cradle to his grave, and though his loves were sometimes evanescent. they were to him terribly real while they lasted. Before he was ten years old he literally fell in love with his cousin, Mary Duff, whose marriage six years later almost threw him into convulsions ; at the age of thirteen he conceived such a passion for another cousin, Margaret Parker, that he could neither eat nor sleep when he expected to see her ; and at fifteen he actually proposed for Mary Chaworth, grand-daughter of the Mr. Chaworth whose death is mentioned above. No doubt these attachments might never have been formed had he been able, like other boys, to lavish his childish love on his mother, and on suitable male companions of his own age and rank ; but unquestionably these romantic escapades had their effect on his after life, and he always believed that he would have been a much better, purer, and happier man if Mary Chaworth had not rejected him. Who can tell?

Entering Trinity College, Cambridge, in 1805, he left it in 1808, without trying, or even caring to try, for any of the usual University distinctions. During this period, however, he spent a year at Southwell, where the genial encouragement of the Pigotts induced him to prepare some youthful effusions for publication, and the *Hours of Idleness* appeared in 1807. It is a common error to suppose that it was the attack of the *Edinburgh Review* on this juvenile crudity that hurried him into literature; the *Hours* appeared early in 1807, the *Review* attack was made (it is supposed by Lord Brougham) a year later, and it was not till a year after the *Review* article that he replied to it, and his other hostile critics, in the satirical poem, *English Bards and Scotch Reviewers.* Moreover, six months before the adverse criticism, he told Miss Piggott that, besides other "scribbling," he had a short satire ready to be published soon, and it was this satire he afterwards elaborated into his reply. The fact is, that the insatiate thirst for applause had taken such possession of him as to preclude the possibility of his seriously bidding farewell to poetry. The satire is of little permanent interest, or value, but it took at the time, and that was quite enough to satisfy at once his thirst for vengeance and for fame.

In 1809, accompanied by his friend, John Cam Hobhouse, he visited the continent of Europe, wandering for two years through the romantic and historic scenery of Spain, and the Turkish dependencies in Greece, Albania, and Asia Minor. His biographer, the celebrated Irish poet, Thomas Moore, describes the settled melancholy that surrounded him before, during, and after his continental tour, but neither Moore, nor any other of the numerous writers on the subject, has given an adequate cause for the gloomy sadness that habitually attended him. It is sheer nonsense to suppose that a man of twenty-one, who had led what would be now considered a most studious life, and who had already succeeded in making himself the dreaded exposer of the shallow critics of the day, could have been at the same time leading such a recklessly dissipated life as to have, at that early age, shattered his constitution, physically and morally. That he had not done so mentally is abundantly proved by the surpassing excellence of the first and second cantos of *Childe Harold*, the publication of which, shortly after his return to England, immediately lifted him to the position of first living poet of England ; "I awoke one morning and found myself famous," is his own pithy summing up of the verdict of his contemporaries.

The success of *Childe Harold* was due to many causes, the more obvious of which were these three:—First, the subject of these cantos possessed a vital interest for every reader, not only in Great Britain, but throughout Europe, for all were watching, with absorbing interest, the Titanic struggle then going on in the scene of Childe Harold's pilgrimage; secondly, the manner in which Byron handled his themes showed that he was imbued with the spirit of the age in every fibre of his soul, that he was emphatically the poet of the nineteenth century revolt against the ideas of the eighteenth ; and lastly, the public, in spite of his protestations, insisted on identifying the poet with his hero, and eagerly sought for what they were eager to believe were incidents in the career of the only poet who had fully shown that he was thoroughly awake to the fact that he was living in one of the most momentous periods in the history of the world.

For the next few years, 1812-1816, Byron was one of the "lions" of society ; but that he was very far from being the mere dissipated rake that he is generally supposed to have been is abundantly proved by the rapidity with which he issued his series of Eastern Tales during these years. The *Giaour* (pronounced *Djour*, to rhyme with *hour*), and the *Bride of Abydos*, appeared in 1813; the *Corsair* and *Lara*, in 1814 ; the *Siege of Corinth* and *Parisina* early in 1816. In these productions, also, the public were anxious to identify the author with his heroes, and Byron was no longer unwilling to foster the illusion—it helped to account for the air of haughty restraint by which he strove to mask his extreme shyness in society, a shyness that he could not overcome and would not acknowledge ; and it gratified his morbid desire to be thought worse than he really was.

During this period, also, unfortunately for himself and his posthumous character, he married. In November, 1813, he proposed for Miss Milbanke and was rejected, she, however, making the strange request to be privileged to correspond with him. In September, 1814, he again proposed, and this time he was accepted. The marriage took place on January 2nd, 1815, and never has there been a more ill-assorted union. She was a most exemplary woman, he was not an exemplary man ; she was a professional philanthropist, he shrank, morbidly almost, from letting his right hand know what his left hand was doing in the way of generosity ; she had the ambition of reforming a rake, and seems to have married him for no other purpose, he did not want to be reformed, and revolted from the very first against such open means of conversion as his wife desired to employ ; she was calm, cold, serene, and unforgiving, he was stormy, fiery, restless, and the most placable of men ; she wanted him to turn over to the rationalism and formalism of the eighteenth century, he was in stormy revolt against the meaningless insipidity of the past, and was indeed the prophet of the turbulent nineteenth century; she had so little appreciation of her husband's fame that she wanted him "to give up the bad habit of making verses," he felt the afflatus of the poet in every pulsation of his heart, and his poetic fame was to him as the very breath of his nostrils. With characters so diametrically opposite it would have been impossible for them to live happily together under the most favorable circumstances. But apart from their incompatibility of temper, there were other causes to keep them from agreeing. Byron's creditors began to dun him unmercifully almost from the day of his marriage, and there were no fewer than nine executions put into the house within the year ; he was habitually melancholy, and his keenly sensitive nature had suffered acutely from the death of several of his most intimate friends, so that his moodiness, aggravated by pecuniary embarrassment and a bitter sense of isolation, rendered him daily more and more irritable, and made him more and more feel the utter want of sympathy between himself and his even-tempered wife. She, indeed, had little feeling for whims and caprices of any kind, and when Byron implored her to dismiss her maid, whom he suspected and hated with all the intensity of his fiery nature, she met his request by promoting Mrs. Clermont to the position of companion and confidante.

On January 15th, 1816, Lady Byron left him to visit her parents, taking with her their infant daughter, Augusta Ada ; on the way she wrote her "Dear Duck" a most affectionate letter, signed, "Your Pippin;" a few days later her father, Sir Ralph Milbanke, wrote to him saying that she would never return, and she herself confirmed the statement shortly afterwards. She had consulted Dr. Baillie as to her husband's sanity, had informed her parents that she wished for a separation, had submitted her case to Dr. Lushington (an eminent legal authority), and had afterwards had an interview with him in order to strengthen her position, had bound her legal adviser to a secrecy which he never violated, and being thus armed at all points she proposed a separation, to which Byron consented, and the deed of separation was drawn up the month after her desertion of her unhappy husband. These are all the *facts* that have ever been *ascertained* in relation to the separation, and the real causes which led to it are to-day as little *known* as they were at the time of its consummation. Lady Byron had bound Dr. Lushington to secrecy, so that the only person who could have told what her allegations were at the time was forever silenced. Byron's friend, Hobhouse, was delegated to ascertain the causes, and he "racked his brains" in suggesting queries, going even so far as to ask if she accused him of murder or incest, to all of which he received a positive denial, delivered with an angelic sweetness and the air of a not yet sainted martyr who had suffered an irreparable wrong. The denials by herself, and the pledges of secrecy imposed upon others, did not, however, prevent her from imagining the foulest and most diabolical slander against her husband and his sister ; and years afterwards, when he was in his grave and could not answer them, she made these charges a frequent topic of conversation in her coterie of scandal-mongering lady friends, notwithstanding the fact that she had, in the interval, lived on terms of the closest intimacy with the sister implicated in the atrocious accusation. A distinguished authoress on this continent, to whose family the curses of unsubstantiated charges subsequently came home to roost, made it her business, some years ago, to blazon the statements of Lady Byron to the world, with the unlooked-for effect of vastly increasing the circulation of Byron's works, and convincing the vast majority of readers that the charges were utterly destitute of truth, and that the causes of the separation are still as much a subject of speculation as ever.

Shortly after the separation an indiscreet friend published Byron's *Farewell* (the manuscript of which, Moore tells us, was all blurred and blotted by the fast-falling tears of the lonely and embittered poet); and this, together with the publication of the *Sketch* (in which Mrs. Clermont was lashed with an unsparing hand, as the insidious cause of the domestic trouble), gave the penny-a-liners of the day an excuse for an unprecedented outpouring of venom and scurrilous abuse. The public took the side of the wife, Byron was made the scape-goat for the immoralities of the nation, and he who had so lately been the idol of the crowd dared not show his face in the streets without incurring the risk of personal violence at the hands of the fickle mob.

He left England in April, 1816, and never afterwards took up his residence in the land of his birth. He passed through Flanders, visited Switzerland, and removed to Venice in November, 1816, where he resided till near the close of the year 1819. Though his life during these three years was neither virtuous nor happy, it cannot have been so wholly given up to debauchery as is commonly asserted ; for he completed the third canto of *Childe Harold* in July, 1816, *Manfred* in February, the fourth canto of *Childe Harold* in June, and *Beppo* in October. 1817 ; the *Ode to Venice* in July, the first canto of *Don Juan* in September, *Mazeppa* in October, and the second canto of *Don Juan* in December, 1818 ; and the third and fourth cantos of *Don Juan* in November, 1819. Besides writing all these he was at the same time carrying on a lengthy correspondence with his publisher, John Murray, his letters being amongst the finest productions of this kind in the language.

Early in the year 1819 Byron became acquainted with the Countess Guiccioli, daughter of Count Gamba, and wife of another Count, who was complacent enough to agree to a separation in order that his Countess might openly form a *liaison* with the English lord. From this time forward (January, 1820) she and her father occupied apartments in the house of her paramour, who would indeed have been equally willing to be her husband, but he could not, and Lady Byron would not, procure a divorce. However much we may deplore the immorality of this connection, it was unquestionably a good thing for Byron. It to some degree satisfied his passionate craving for sympathy, and the Countess did everything in her power to stimulate the poetic genius that his wife had held so cheaply. The mere catalogue of works written during this period shows how great must have been his industry as well as his ability. No poet has ever produced a greater amount of good work in the same time than Byron did during the three years of his residence with the Gambas at Ravenna, Pisa, and Genoa.

The Countess and her father were ardent lovers of liberty, and it was probably due to their influence, as much as to his appointment as a member of the London Greek Committee, that Byron resolved to take an active part in aid of the Greeks, who were then engaged in their memorable struggle for independence. Accordingly he set out for Greece towards the close of the year 1823, full of the ardent enthusiasm and love of liberty that formed such prominent features in his character. He was, however, doomed to disappointment. The Greeks had no plans, and the troops seemed more anxious for their pay than for the success of their cause ; he was detained for five months at Cephalonia, trying, not altogether in vain, to bring order out of the chaos of discordant elements; he reached Missolonghi in December, only to find the same pretentious arrogance among the chiefs, the same mercenary spirit among their followers, that had well nigh worried him to death at Cephalonia ; he took the command of an expedition against Lepanto, but before the expedition could start the malaria of the marshes had seized on his frame, and at the very crisis of his fate the valiant Suliotes mutinied for their pay. Count Gamba, the veteran advocate of liberty, was present with the Englishman, his son-in-law in all but in law, and he describes the intrepid conduct of the dying hero when the mercenary Greeks burst into his apartment, demanding their pay with furious

threats, and found themselves literally cowed by the cool and resolute courage with which they were confronted; "a more undaunted
man in the hour of peril never breathed," was the verdict of the
chivalrous old regenerator, whose plots for the freedom of Italy had
inured him to perils of no ordinary kind, and had well qualified
him to give an authoritative verdict on such a subject. But undaunted courage could not avert the stroke of the fell destroyer ;
and on the 19th of April, 1824, in view of the promised land of his
own redemption and regeneration, the greatest writer of the century forever ceased to work.

The announcement of his death, at the early age of thirty-six,
came with a shock to the knowledge of his countrymen, and not
only of them, but of all Europe ; and men began speedily to ask
themselves, with a keen pang of remorse, had they not been too
hasty in their verdict of condemnation ? Could one who had done
so much literary work of the highest order, in so brief a space,
have been the reckless profligate they had been so willing to consider him ? Could he, who had embodied in himself and had expressed the spirit of the nineteenth century as no other poet either
could or would have done, who had lifted men's minds from the contemplation of the dead bones of the past, had raised them above the
horrors of the present, and had pointed them to the possibilities of
emancipated intelligence in the future,—could he have been the
heartless, soulless, sensual misanthrope he had been believed to be
when he had been driven in anger and disgrace from England only
eight short years before. Men have ceased to ask some of these
questions already, and the calmer verdict of the present is that he
was more sinned against than sinning.

His services to literature were by no means inconsiderable. Pope
had set the example of writing true poetry in a diction marked by
the utmost carefulness of syntax and prosody, and a school of
poetasters had arisen, who imitated Pope's versification and would
fain have made the world believe, with them, that correctness of
form was the essential requisite in poetry. Byron was an ardent
admirer of Pope, but had the most unqualified contempt for his
mere imitators ; and he showed by his earlier works that a vivid
interpretation of nature was by no means inconsistent with correctness of versification, and by his later works that fidelity to nature
must far transcend mere correctness of expression. Scott, and
others before him, had revolted against the fashion of rationalistic
formalism in poetry ; Coleridge, Southey, Rogers, Campbell, and
Wordsworth, not less than Keats, Shelley, and Byron, had entered
a practical protest in favor of the new ideas heralded by the French
Revolution ; but of all the members of this galaxy of poetical stars
Byron was preeminently at once the prophet and the interpreter of

the new ideas. In the tumult and doubt of the first years of the century, he, and he alone, never flinched from his advocacy of the principles of tolerance and freedom which were then the subjects of debate and strife in every quarter of the globe. He won his first laurels with the opening cantos of *Childe Harold*, in which, with true poetic instinct, he dealt with themes and scenes on which all thoughtful men were pondering; and even in his succeeding *Eastern Tales*, though the personages were alien, the thoughts and language were the expression of the ideas of millions of his age. While every other English poet was dealing with themes of the past, Byron plunged boldly into the turbid stream of the present; and his overwhelming success should teach us that the surest way to reach the heart of the people is to present them with glowing poetical pictures of that in which they are most deeply interested. Byron was intensely subjective, feeling deeply, and identifying himself thoroughly with all that he described; he was deficient in dramatic power in so far that he could not describe vividly what he could not feel, but in his portraiture of character he invariably tried to project himself into the situation, and to describe what he believed would have been his own sensations under similar conditions. Hence, though he never could have produced a true drama, many of his characters, scenes, and situations are marked by an almost appalling dramatic force and interest. It has been the custom to identify him with the heroes of his creation, and to say that they are all portraits of the same satanic model under different names ; but it surely is a very shallow criticism that cannot detect differences, and very marked ones, between the *Giaour* and *Don Juan*, *Lara* and *Childe Harold*, *Manfred* and the *Corsair*. He was fond of identifying himself with his sensational heroes during his brief career as a lion of London society, because the public would have it so, and he found it an excellent mask for the bashfulness that cost him so many pangs ; but that he was far from being the blood-stained, callous, relentless debauchee of his works is abundantly proved by the evidences of his industry, and by the prudence, sagacity, and energy displayed by him during the sad closing scene of his not inglorious career.

THE ISLES OF GREECE.

In the third canto of *Don Juan* the hero is ship-wrecked and cast ashore on one of the Cyclades (a group of islands in the Grecian Archipelago); here he is found, carried into a cave, and tenderly nursed by the pirate chieftain's daughter Haidee, one of the sweetest and purest creations of Byron's poetic fancy. The pirate's long absence on an excursion having induced the belief that he was

dead, Haidee and Don Juan are married, and during the marriage
festivities this lyric poem is chanted by a wandering minstrel. It
is far from being the best of Byron's lyrics, but it exhibits some of
his characteristics in a marked degree, and the subject will make
it popular long after better productions of its author have passed
into oblivion. The special fault of Byron's genius—his want of
true dramatic insight—is visible ; the thoughts are not such as
would have occurred to a Greek minstrel, had such a character existed : they are exactly the thoughts of Byron himself projected
into the position of an itinerant bard. In reading the poem it is
well to bear this in mind: it is Byron himself who is speaking, but
it is Byron masquerading in the disguise of an old poet, of such a
poet as Homer might have been. In fact, the introduction of such
a character is an anachronism ; though the personification is fairly
well sustained throughout. The poem also exhibits Byron's special
excellence, though not so markedly as do some of his other lyrics.
He was emphatically the exponent of the thought of the nineteenth
century, of that strong spirit of revolt against feudalism that began
with the American War of Independence, culminated in the overthrow of so many tyrannies by Napoleon, the greatest tyrant of
his own or any other age, and can not be said to have ceased in
our own time, when Nihilism and Socialism are waging energetic
war against the abuses of misgovernment.

Where burning Sappho loved and sung.—The lyric
poetess, Sappho, was born about 625, B.C., in Mitylené, the
principal city in the island of Lesbos. She wrote hymns, elegies,
and love songs of unusual warmth, all of which are lost, except an
ode to Venus, and a few fragments of her other poems. The story
of her love for Phaon, and her suicide by plunging into the sea
from the "lover's leap" at Leucadia (Santa Maura), is well known,
though very probably untrue. The Sapphic metre still preserves
her name; it was invented by her, and has been imitated by many
poets from Horace to Canning, whose "Needy Knife-Grinder" is
familiar to most readers of our satirical squibs.

Delos rose—out of the Ægean sea by command of Neptune in
order to afford a haven of rest to Leda in her flight from the vengeance of Juno, whom she had temporarily supplanted in the
affections of Jupiter. **Phœbus sprung**—into existence with
his twin-sister Diana as the offspring of this amour. The myth
attributing the birth of Phœbus (Apollo), or the Sun, and Diana
(Luna), or the Moon, to an amour of Jupiter (Sanscrit Dhyupitri)
= Light Father is common to all the branches of the Aryan family.

The Scian and the Teian muse—The island of Chios
(Scio), besides claiming the honor of being Homer's birthplace
(see notes on Addison), was celebrated in historic times for the

attention paid by its inhabitants to the study of rhetoric and history. The town of Teos on the coast of Asia Minor was the birthplace of Anacreon, the witty writer of love and drinking songs that have been often imitated,—perhaps most successfully by Thomas Moore, the immortal author of the Irish Melodies.

The hero's harp, the lover's lute—Note the peculiar beauty of the alliteration,—so strong and masculine in the aspirates, so soft and dulcet in the liquids. The harp refers to Homer, the lute to Anacreon.

Which echo further west, &c.—Moore naïvely speaks of the delight with which he and Byron had learned of the warm welcome accorded in America to a pirated edition of their then published works ; and it is quite possible that the allusion in the text refers to this mark of appreciation.

" Islands of the Blest "—In Homer and other Cyclic poets the Earth is surrounded by a broad river, the Ocean, and on the western shore of this "swiftly flowing" stream are the "Islands of the Blest," identified by geographers of a later age with the Canary Islands.

The mountains look on Marathon—is certainly more poetic than was Byron's first draft of the line, viz.: " Euboea looks on Marathon." The accounts of the battles of Marathon, Salamis, and Platoea should be read in some History of Greece. Marathon is mentioned in Homer : it was a small village on the east coast of Attica, about twenty miles N.E. of Athens. Mount Pentelicus and Mount Parnes look on it. On the plain of Marathon, B. C. 490, the Persian host of Darius, under Datis and Artaphernos, was defeated by the Greeks under Miltiades. The recalling of the glories of Marathon was not in vain ; for here the Greeks, in 1824, five years later than the writing and three years later than the publication of the poem, defeated an army of the Turks. **The Persian's grave**—is probably, by a pardonable confusion of thought, the celebrated *tumulus* erected in honor of the fallen Greeks.

A king—rocky brow—sea-born Salamis—The king was Xerxes, the son and successor of Darius. Ten years after the battle of Marathon (480 B. C.) he invaded Greece with an army of over five millions of men, including camp-followers, defeated the Greeks under Leonidas at Thermopylae, was defeated in the sea fight of Salamis by the Athenians under Themistocles and Aristides, and fled back in terror to Asia, leaving his general Mardonius to be defeated at Platoea, 479, B. C. He was an eye witness of the destruction of his fleet at Salamis, being seated on a throne on "the rocky brow" of Mount Ægaleos on the mainland. "Sea-born Salamis," now *Koluri*, is a rocky island forming a natural breakwater for the harbor of Eleusis : there was another Salamis, a city founded by Teucer, in the island of Cyprus, and alluded to by Horace. Is *sate* a legitimate archaism ? Byron was fond of trying such forms for effect, notwithstanding the fact that he was regarded by Gifford, the eminent critic of the London *Quarterly Review*, as the purest writer of English among the poets of the time.

And when the sun set, where were they ?—Mark the effect of the suddenness of the question ; and compare it with the sudden change in the last line of the poem.

The heroic lay—a common synonym for poetry, or poem. Cf. Scott's *Lay of the Last Minstrel;* the word is of Celtic origin, but is akin to the German *lied.* Note the abruptness of the transitions, the metaphors, and other rhetorical devices, the strongly-marked antitheses, and the appropriateness of the classical allusions; these are all characteristic of the old ballads imitated here by Byron.

Link'd among a fetter'd race—With the fall of Byzantium (Constantinople) in 1453, perished the freedom of Greece ; nor was it recovered till a few years after the writing of this poem. *Link'd*, A. S. *hline; fetter'd*, literally having a shackle on the *foot.* Cf. the Greek πέδη.

For Greeks a blush—for Greece a tear—Why is the distinction made ?

Three hundred—There were only 300 Spartans present at the battle of Thermopylæ, but the auxiliaries brought the total number up to somewhat over a thousand. *Thermopylæ* was a pass in the south-east of Thessaly, one of the northern provinces of Ancient Greece; it was enclosed between Mount Œta and the Maliac Gulf (*Zeitoun*). In the Greek War of Independence an unimportant engagement took place here so that "a new Thermopylæ" was formed to some extent.

What, silent still ? and silent all ?—Supply the ellipsis.

Let one living head, &c.—The career of Marco Bozzaris, the great Suliote leader, seems almost the fulfilment of this prayer. Note the somewhat peculiar use of the word *but* in this and the preceding stanza. Read Halleck's spirited poem, *Marco Bozzaris.*

Samian wine—Scio's vine—Samos, Chios, and other islands of the Ægean were celebrated for the excellence of their wines. Note the sarcasm in the last three lines of the stanza ! *Bacchanal,* a worshipper of Bacchus, the Greek and Roman god of wine.

You have the Pyrrhic dance as yet, &c.—Note the uses of *you* and *ye* in this stanza, and also the colloquial *as yet.* Byron seems to have overlooked the fact that the Pyrrhic dance cannot claim the same parentage as the Pyrrhic phalanx, the former being invented by Pyrrhichus, and the latter being so much improved from the old Macedonian phalanx by Pyrrhus, king of Epirus, as to have his name associated with it as though he had been the inventor. The phalanx is as old as Homer, and is a name applied to the serried formation of troops from the fanciful resemblance to *rollers* (phalanges) following each other in rapid and uniform succession. The dance was of the usual kind of war dances common to all warlike, semi-civilized nations; it was a gymnastic performance rather than a dance in the modern sense of the term.

Cadmus—the Phœnician (or Egyptian, according to another form of the legend), founded Thebes, the capital of Bœotia, about 1450 B. C. and introduced writing into Greece, by making known the Phœnician alphabet of sixteen letters, which was finally perfected by the poet Simonides. See Haydn's *Dictionary of Dates.*

Polycrates—the tyrant of Samos, and patron of Anacreon, was crucified by the Persian satrap, or governor, of Sardis, B. C. 522.

A tyrant; but our masters then, &c.—The word *tyrant* is used here in its Greek sense, i.e. an irresponsible ruler; it is connected with the older form κοίρανος, derived from κάρα = the head, and thus means nothing more than *chief*, or head man. The natural tendency of irresponsibility to degenerate into cruelty has given the word its present meaning, just as the word *despot* has changed from its original meaning of *master* into its present meaning of *cruel master*. Is there any difference between "our masters then" and "our then masters?"

The Chersonese—The Greek Chersonnesus, or Cherronnesus, means literally a dry land island, i.e. a peninsula. The term was applied to many other peninsulas besides the Tauric Chersonnesus to which it here refers. Miltiades, son of Cimon, after defeating the Persians (*see above*), died ingloriously in prison at Athens, of a wound received in a semi-piratical expedition against the island of Paros.

Another despot of the kind.—The word *despot*, like tyrant, originally meant nothing more than *master*, Gr. δεσπότης, from the root *pot* = powerful, appearing in Gr. πόσις, ποτνία, Lat. *potens*. Skeat says the origin of the *des* is unknown; it is probably derived from the Gr. δέω = to bind, cf. δεσμός (*desmos*), a link,—so that the *despot* = the chief whose *power binds* the tribe together. **Kind**, A.S. *cynd:* the adjective is of the same origin. cf. Gr. and Lat. γένος, genus. Shakspeare's "A little more than *kin*, but less than *kind*," is a happy play on the etymology of the word.

On Suli's rock and Parga's shore.—*Suli* is a mountainous district in the south of the pashalik of Janina, or Epirus. The Suliotes, a mixed race, Albanian and Greek, were reduced to subjection in 1801 by Ali Pasha, after a stubborn resistance of fifteen years. In 1820 (the year after the composition of this ode) they vigorously supported their former opponents against the Turks, and greatly distinguished themselves by their bravery, and, if the truth must be told, by their mercenary turbulence. (See biographical sketch above.) *Parga* is a fortified town on the coast of Albania, south-west of Janina, and north-west of the entrance to the gulf of Arta.

The Doric mother's bore.—The Spartans were the most renowned and warlike of the Dorians, who were in ancient times the most warlike of the Greek tribes. The terrible heroism of the dames of ancient Sparta is well illustrated in the following fragment :—

> " A Spartan, his companions slain,
>   Alone from battle fled :
> His mother, kindling with disdain
>   That she had borne him, struck him dead ;
> For courage, and not birth alone,
>   In Sparta constitutes a son."

The Heracleidan blood.—The descendants of Herakles (Hercules), having been expelled from the Peloponnesus (Morea), appealed for aid to the Dorians, by whom the " Return of the Herakleidæ " was triumphantly achieved. The story belongs to the purely mythical age, but the subsequent bravery of the Doric Spartans is matter of history.

Trust not for freedom to the Franks, &c.—Louis XVIII. was at this time King of France, and Byron seems to have held him in the most undisguised contempt; but here he probably alludes to the former intrigues of Ali Pasha with Napoleon, a partnership in treachery that boded ill for the liberties of Greece. Napoleon's career was now ended, it is true, but Byron may have thought it well to warn the Greek patriots against being hemmed in at once by " Turkish force, and Latin fraud."

Our virgins dance—the Romaika, a favorite measure said to be derived from the Pyrrhic dance of ancient days.

Tear-drop laves—slaves.—Is this a perfect rhyme? Note the beauty of the alliteration in this and the concluding stanza.

Sunium's marbled steep = the southern promontory of Attica, on which stood a celebrated temple of Athena, the patron goddess of Athens. The *marble columns* of the temple, now in ruins, have given to the cape its modern name of Cape Colonné.

Swan-like, let me sing and die.—The well-known fable that the swan sings her own funeral dirge, on feeling the symptoms of her approaching dissolution, has always been a favorite theme with poets. The introduction of the allusion here is very graceful, placed as it is, in the mouth of the patriotic old bard who felt that the continued enslavement of his country would be his own death-knell. Observe the abruptness of the ending of the poem; it is quite in the style of the old ballad poetry of all nations.

THOMAS ARNOLD, D.D.—1795-1842.

UNTHOUGHTFULNESS—Extract XLV., page 227.

Biographical sketch.—The name of Arnold is so familiar, and so many of the name have made themselves less or more celebrated in literature, criticism, and education, that it is not altogether unnecessary to guard the youthful reader against confounding one Arnold with another. Dr. Arnold, the greatest of modern school-masters, must not be confounded with the Rev. T. K. Arnold, author of several school-books dealing chiefly with classical composition; nor with Edwin Arnold, the gifted author of *The Light of Asia;* nor with his own son, Matthew Arnold, the critic, essayist, poet, and Inspector of National Schools; nor with another son, Thomas Arnold, the talented author of an excellent Manual of English Literature.

Thomas Arnold was born in 1795, at West Cowes, Isle of Wight, where his father held the position of collector of customs. Receiving his early education from a painstaking aunt, he went to Winchester at the age of twelve, and four years later matriculated and obtained a scholarship at Corpus Christi College, Oxford. At the University he enjoyed the friendship of Whately, afterwards Archbishop of Dublin; and his manly rectitude of conduct and of character secured him the respect and esteem of all his contemporaries. Seldom has there lived a man who had less of the outward show of a saint, but seldom indeed has there been one more deeply imbued with the essence of true religion. It pervaded his whole life, and it irresistibly influenced the lives of all with whom he came in contact.

He left Oxford in 1819, and settled at Laleham, near Staines, where, for the next nine years, he spent his time chiefly in superintending the studies of youths preparing for the University, and, during the last year or two, in historical studies on the lines laid down by Niebuhr in his Roman History, 1827. The head-mastership of Rugby, one of the great Public schools of England, becoming vacant, Arnold was induced to apply for the position, and in December, 1827, he was elected. In the month of August following he entered on his new duties, and it is not too much to say that never has a wiser choice been made by the trustees of any institution of learning. In one of his testimonials it was predicted that if elected "he would change the face of education all through the Public schools of England." He did so, but he did far more; he revolutionized the scholastic profession, and introduced a system of discipline that has been productive of the greatest and most lasting benefit throughout the schools of Christendom. A brief sketch of his peculiar method will be found in Extract LXXII., page 350, from the pen of one of his favorite pupils ; but perhaps a better idea of the effect produced by the new mode of discipline at Rugby will be gathered from the pages of that admirable book for boys, *Tom Brown's School Days*, by Tom Hughes, another of Dr. Arnold's Rugby boys.

A *History of Rome*, a well annotated edition of *Thucydides*, and some volumes of *Sermons* and *Lectures*, are enough to show how great a name Arnold might have made for himself in literature, had he devoted himself exclusively to a literary career. In 1841 he was appointed, by Lord Melbourne, to the professorship of Modern History at Oxford ; but he had only delivered a few lectures when he was suddenly cut off in the very prime of life by an attack of *angina pectoris*, one of the most excruciating of diseases. He died on the 12th of June, 1842, and was buried under the altar in the chancel of Rugby chapel.

UNTHOUGHTFULNESS.

Arnold's sermons, preached to the Rugby boys in the chapel attached to the school, are models of what sermons to boys ought to be ; and the present discourse is an excellent example of his usual style when addressing the pupils in their collective capacity. The school sermons were rather familiar lectures than formal sermons ; they treated of all topics on which it was right that the hearers should be warned or instructed ; and they dealt with these topics in such a way that many a pupil who would have been repelled by the formalism of a regular sermon, found himself irresistibly attracted by the simplicity, the earnestness, and the moral grandeur of the arguments addressed to his understanding, and appealing, at every step, to his higher and better nature. Arnold never talked over the heads of his audience on the one hand, nor did he fall into the opposite, and no less hurtful, extreme of treating his young hearers as babes, incapable of understanding sound reasoning on topics of the last importance. The object aimed at in this lecture was one very near and dear to the heart of the Rugby headmaster— the cultivation among his boys of "a spirit of manly, and, much more of Christian thoughtfulness." The development of individual character he held to be the most important function of a great Public school ; and the noble example of manly piety that he gave in his own daily life, supplemented by the chapel lectures, did more to raise the moral tone of the school than all the other influences that had been brought to bear on this object.

Note the clearness with which the several propositions are enunciated in the lecture, and the conclusiveness of the reasoning by

C

which they are established. Sharp antitheses are characteristic of the style, and several climaxes lend point and interest to the reasoning. Observe, also, that he does not attempt to wheedle or cajole his pupils into a pretended love of the right, and see how affectionately he reckons himself as one of them, "*we must beware of excess,*" etc. A careful study of the extract will repay the reader, and in connection with it the extract from Dean Stanley's Life, commencing on page 350, may be read with great advantage.

Folly.—The etymology of the word is significant; it is derived from an old French word, *fol* (*fou*), and that from Lat. *follis*= *bellows,*—so that the *fool* is literally a *wind-bag.*

Most universal evils—*Universal* is used here in the sense of *wide-spread,* but the word should not be compared. Why not? Note the abruptness with which the speaker plunges at once *in medias res,* and how, having thus arrested the attention at the outset, he rivets it by the amplification of his definition—**it takes in.** In what sense is this phrase employed here?

Clever, prudent, sensible, thoughtful, and wise.— Show by an exact definition of each word that this is a true climax. *Clever* is a corruption of an old English adjective, *deliver* = nimble, and has possibly assumed its present spelling from being confounded with another old word, *cliver* = ready to seize. The derivation given in Webster is untenable.

Confusion between ignorance and innocence.— Language abundantly illustrates the extent to which this confusion has prevailed, though in a direction somewhat different from Arnold's view; the word *innocent,* for example, which is literally= *not injuring,* has come to be used as a synonym for a *fool,* as though the right use of reason were to enable us to injure one another. *Simpleton, silly,* and many other words, afford examples of the same tendency.

You do not lessen, &c.,—the indefinite second person presents the thought more forcibly than the common, *one does not,* &c.

Wisdom—cunning—the distinction is well brought out in the text,—*wisdom* being =*wise doom,* i.e., wise judgment, discretion ; whereas *cunning* (A.S. *cunnan*=to know) is merely knowing, and is applied with equal propriety to the knowingness of the fox, and to the craftiness of the savage. Whether the madman is as cunning in real life as he is represented in sensational fiction is at least doubtful.

Mark the deep earnestness and directness of application to the various characters of boys throughout the remainder of the lecture.

Notions of boys, about what is right and wrong.— Nothing gave Arnold greater trouble in his work of reformation at Rugby than the foolish prejudices of the boys, fostered by the tra-

ditions of the school. Readers of *Tom Brown* will see the mar-
vellous tact, patience, and firmness with which the Doctor combated
these "foolish, commonplace notions."

Works of amusement.—If it was necessary to warn the
boys at Rugby against works that were "not wicked for the most
part," how much more necessary is it now to guard against the
fatal influence of the "books of downright wickedness," so common
at the present day !

Gorged = stuffed to repletion, Lat. *gurges* = throat. The
metaphor is taken from the habits of the lower animals, and of
savages.

The remedy rests—with each of you individually—
this is exactly in accordance with Arnold's plan of dealing with
evil at Rugby ; instead of foolishly trying to stamp it out by his
own authority, he appeals to the higher nature of his hearers, reminds them of their "responsibility in the sight of God," and then
leaves the matter with Him and their own awakened consciences.

WILLIAM CULLEN BRYANT—1794-1872.

To the Evening Wind—Extract LVI., page 272.

Biographical Sketch.—In the year 1808, the year following the publication of Byron's *Hours of Idleness*, a small volume of poems was published in Boston, consisting of *The Embargo, or Sketches of the Times, a Satire*, and the *Spanish Revolution*, with some minor poems. The muster-roll of American poets did not then contain so many names as it does now, and the appearance of a new aspirant for fame was gladly welcomed ; but when it became known that the author was a child of only thirteen years the welcome was heightened by the public anticipation of what ought to be achieved by one whose mere infancy had given such unmistakable marks of genius. The child was WILLIAM CULLEN BRYANT, born at Cummington, in Massachusetts, in 1794 ; and the brilliant promise of his childhood was fully sustained by his *Thanatopsis*, the publication of which, five years later, at once raised him to the front rank of American poets, and entitled him to an honorable place among the poets of all ages. In 1821, *The Ages* added to his reputation ; but circumstances then directed his energies into other channels, and since that time he has only added an occasional minor poem to the productions of his youthful muse. Simplicity and naturalness in the thought, correctness of expression, and purity of imagery are among his more prominent characteristics as a poet; while as a prose writer his style is at once pure, easy, and idiomatic beyond what might have been expected from one whom circumstances compelled to write so much.

He was educated at Williams College, was called to the bar in 1815, and practised law for ten years, chiefly at West Barrington, Mass. In 1825 he removed to the City of New York, where he became editor of the *Review*, and subsequently, in 1826, editor of the *Evening Post*, of which he was one of the proprietors. This latter position he held till the time of his death, and during his occupancy of the editorial chair he did more than any man of his time to elevate the standard of journalism. Being singularly free from jealousy, he encouraged and secured the co-operation of journalistic talent wherever he could find it, and thus, having associated with himself an exceptionally brilliant staff of contributors, he made the *Evening Post* to be a power in the land, not only in politics, but in literature. He hated slip-shod English, and drew up for the guidance of contributors an *Index Expurgatorius* of tabooed words and phrases, that has almost attained to the rank of a final authority. In politics he was an ardent lover and uncompromising advocate of the principles of a free soil and free institutions; hence he was an almost bitter opponent of the slavery institutions of the Southern States, and a powerful upholder of the Union cause during the American civil war.

Having lived to see the triumph of the principles for which he had long and ably contended, he died full of years and honors, in the year 1872, having almost reached the three score years and ten allotted as the limit of the span of life.

TO THE EVENING WIND.

The *ottava rima* in which this ode is written was adopted by English writers from the Italians. Tasso and Ariosto employed it as their heroic metre, though lines of eleven syllables (endecasyllabic) are frequent with them and other Italian poets. Byron's *Don Juan* is the best example of its use in English literature. In this extract it may be noticed that Bryant's intense desire to employ only the purest of English occasionally makes him sacrifice the metre to the necessities of the language : he never leaves us in doubt as to what he wishes to express, and he employs the plainest and most idiomatic language to convey his meaning ; but his anxiety to write only pure English interferes seriously with the rhythmical structure of his stanzas, and we have to content ourselves with correctness of Syntax at the expense of harmony in Prosody. The scansion of even the first stanza will be enough to illustrate this peculiarity.

The extract also exemplifies a peculiar excellence of Bryant's genius—the power of producing good effects from slender materials. What an abundance of imagery we have in these five stanzas, and all about the mere ebb and flow of the land and sea breezes ! Every one has felt the gracious influence of this "circle of eternal change ;" but it has not been given to every one to express it so gracefully as Bryant has expressed it.

Lattice—a derivative of *lath* (Welsh *llath* = a rod). Note the different effects produced by the evening wind on the waters of the ocean and on those of the land—it is not the cause of the ocean waves, it merely roughens their crests ; but it "curls the still waters of the lakes" (see third stanza).

Till now—Give the exact parsing of these words ; and give other examples of the use of (so-called) adverbs as nouns.

Nor I alone—Thoughtfulness for the comfort and welfare of others was one of the features of Bryant's character. Note the minuteness of the details and the truth to Nature of this and the following stanzas,

Inhale thee, &c.—Cf. Thomson's *Autumn,—ll.* 1312-13.

> " sucks the healthful gale
> Into his freshen'd soul."

Livelier at coming, &c.—Parse *livelier* and *coming*. What rhetorical figures are employed in this stanza ?

Woodbird in his nest, &c.—Explain the use of *his* in this stanza. Define and derive *majestic, innumerable,* and *harmonics.* Show that "the strange deep harmonics" do not mean the tuneful songs of the birds. What is meant by the expression ?

Darkling waters—"Growing dark" is not a legitimate meaning of the word according to its use and derivation. It is properly an adverb = *in the dark,* formed by the addition of the adverbial suffix *ling* to the adjective *dark,* and used adverbially by all our best writers. See Latham's *Handbook.*

Silver head—A.S. *scolfor* is from the same root as the Lat. *sidus,* and is named from its *whiteness.*

Asleep—Does this mean *sleeping,* or *to sleep ?* The word is pure Anglo-Saxon, its original meanings being *benumbed, inactive, drowsy.*

Moisten'd curls—Explain the phrase.

Shall joy—used in its old sense = *rejoice.* Still common in poetry.

Part—The words *part* and *depart* have changed meanings, the latter word being used by Wycliffe in the sense of to *separate,* while *part* is equivalent to *go away*—a sense not unusual in the poets, e.g. Gray has "the knell of parting day." Bryant employs the word correctly.

Circle of eternal change, &c.—Write a note on the causes of the periodical return of the evening sea-breeze.

Sounds and scents—Note the alliteration ; and observe the fidelity to natural laws exhibited in the stanza. The homesick mariner, carried back in dreams to the rustling leaf and running stream by the "sweet odors in the sea-air," is a picture worthy of the pen of any poet of our time.

The wind was a favourite topic of Bryant's muse. In his *October* and the *May Evening* we find close resemblances to some of the ideas in this Ode. For instance, in the *May Evening,* we have:—

> " Where hast thou wandered, gentle gale, to find
>   The perfumes thou dost bring?
> By brooks, that through the winding meadows wind,
>   Or brink of rushy spring ?"

THOMAS CARLYLE.—1795–1881.

DEATH OF THE PROTECTOR.—Extract LVII., page 274.

In the pages of *Fraser's Magazine*, in the years 1833–1834, appeared in serial form one of the most remarkable prose productions of the century ; and as the speculations of *Sartor Resartus* appeared from month to month it became evident that a new literary power had arisen. Byron had been dead nearly ten years, and the young men of the period had begun to discard their Byron neckties and collars, as they had already given over the habit of trying to imagine themselves corsairs and cut-throats. The throne of literature in England was vacant and it was by a large majority of the public assigned to THOMAS CARLYLE, the magazine writer.

He was born in 1795, at Ecclefechan, in Dumfriesshire, Scotland ; educated first at Annan and Kirkcaldy, and afterwards at the University of Edinburgh ; joined the noble army of martyrs as a schoolmaster for four years ; and returned to Edinburgh in 1818 to enter on a literary career by contributing to the pages of Brewster's *Edinburgh Encyclopædia.* For the next three years he was a diligent student of the German language and literature, becoming, indeed, so enamoured of the German mode of thought and of expression that for the remainder of his life he was, consciously or unconsciously, a translator of German into English. In 1821 he returned to the ranks of the teaching profession as a private tutor, and made such good use of his comparative freedom from distracting influences that he was able to produce an excellent translation of Legendre's *Geometry* and a still more excellent rendering of Goëthe's *Wilhelm-Meister,* in addition to a *Life of Schiller,* in 1823. Three years later he married Jane Baillie Welsh, " a singularly gifted woman," he tells us, " who,—for his sake, had voluntarily sacrificed ambition and fortune." One would be glad to be able to record that the poor woman had met her reward in an equally sacrificing disposition on the part of her husband ; but the pages of his *Reminiscences,* edited by his friend and literary executor, the historian Froude, prove conclusively that Carlyle was the same snarling, querulous, scolding malcontent in his domestic relations that his own works show him to have been in his treatment of public subjects. So blinded was he by an overweening egotism, and so completely did he ignore the self-sacrifice of his wife, that he, in a letter to Goëthe, complacently alludes to his retirement to Craigenputtoch, in his native county, to live on a small property *belonging to her,* as a means " to secure the independence through which I could be enabled to remain true to myself." In this state of dependent independence he remained for the next six years, when the success of his *Sartor Resartus* made it advisable for him to remove to Chelsea, one of the many suburbs of London, and there the "Chelsea sage" continued to reside from 1834 till the time of his death in 1881.

The record of his life is the record of his works—of their composition, publication, and reception by the public. For the first ten years of his literary career he had a hard enough time of it ; but the dogged persistence of the man, and the uncouth ruggedness and force of his style finally broke down all opposition, and the number of his imitators became great enough to satisfy the ambition of the new literary king. *The French Revolution, a History*, appeared in 1837, and its publication placed the author immediately in the front rank of historical portrait painters ; the subject was eminently suited to his peculiar powers as a delineator of the more intense traits of character, and the figures in the tragic narrative stand out as vividly and distinctly as though the writer had been personally acquainted with them all. The following year he published a volume of *Miscellanies*, made up from his previous contributions to the *Edinburgh Review* and other magazines. *Chartism* appeared in 1839, and in 1840, *Heroes, Hero-Worship, and the Heroic in History*, a recast of one of a series of his popular lectures delivered in London. In the *Past and Present* of 1843, he showed his acquaintance with the early English chronicles by an admirable paraphrase of that of St. Edmund Bury, written by the monk Jocelin de Brakelonde, recounting the work and worth of Abbot Samson, a hero after Carlyle's heart. The year 1845 gave to the world *Oliver Cromwell's Letters and Speeches, with Elucidations*, in which the memory of the great Protector of the Commonwealth is for the first time in our literature fully vindicated. His admiration of the forcible measures adopted by his hero from necessity, influenced nearly all his later productions ; and we consequently find an almost idolatrous worship of mere brute force, as the panacea for political evil, exhibited in the *Latter-Day Pamphlets* of 1850, in his second great prose epic, *The History of Frederick the Great* (1858–1860), in his inhuman exultation over the downfall of France in the Franco-Prussian war, and in several other Jeremiads in which he lashes his opponents with more than the force and somewhat less than the decency of a Billingsgate fishwoman. In 1851 he published the *Life of John Sterling*, one of the best biographies in the language, and one of the most pleasing of his many works ; it will probably be read with delight by thousands long after the author's more ambitious histories shall have been consigned to the comparative oblivion of the libraries of the learned.

The most acute critic of modern times, Lord Jeffrey, has pointed out that a certain "dreadful earnestness" is the most salient feature in the character of Carlyle. With him the only virtue is Duty, and among the chief duties are Work, Obedience, Sincerity, and Truth. Hatred of Cant, Hypocrisy, Sham, and Charlatanism in all its forms is shown in every page of his works; but it is shown with an intolerance of temper and an obscurity of language that have done much to prevent his works from being as widely read in our day as their undeniable merits entitle them to be read. A writer who conceives that he has a message to deliver to mankind should try to deliver it in a language clear, harmonious, and alluring. Carlyle delivered his message in a language forcible enough and intelligible enough to all who are willing to study the meaning of their author; but he had a lofty scorn for all the graces of composition and would not condescend to write in a language "understanded of the people." The people, therefore, do not read his works, and he who for half a century influenced the opinions, the actions, and the expressions of his fellowmen will in all probability be read and admired by as few as now read the works of his equally obscure contemporary, the poet Browning.

THE DEATH OF THE PROTECTOR.

The extract very fairly illustrates Carlyle's general style; it shows his German mode of thought and expression, his fondness for antithesis, ellipsis, and other strong figures of speech; it exhibits his sublime scorn for all that did not reach his own high standard; and it illustrates his extraordinary skill in depicting the inner depths of such characters as interested him.

Nothing more—The grim humor of the different applications of the phrase is characteristic. Paraphrase the opening sentence so as to show the full force of each of its clauses. Note the use of initial capital letters for the most important words—a habit of Carlyle's derived partly from his German studies, partly from the general practice of the last century, but chiefly from his own overweening egotism and self-assertion. All rules for the use of capitals and other matters of a like kind are of course more or less arbitrary; but if every writer were to follow his own sweet will as Carlyle has done, there would soon be an end of everything like system in our language, systemless enough already in all conscience.

God's message—is a literal translation of the word *Gospel* and much more accurate than the common rendering of the word, which does not, as generally supposed, simply mean *good story*, but *God story*—the confusion having arisen from the close resemblance of the A. S. *God*—deity, and *god*—good, and also from a not unnatural tendency to distort the word into a translation of the Greek εὐαγγέλιον = good message.

This summer of 165 had been marked by Turenne's surrender of Dunkirk to Lockhart, after the brilliant victory of Cromwell's troops at the battle of the Dunes. Four years later Charles II. rendered himself for ever infamous by selling this much-coveted seaport to the Grand Monarque, Louis XIV.

Thenceforth he enters the Eternities is certainly not English. Translate the clause into English ; and write a note on the use of the historic present tense, and of the plural.

Fifty-nine last April.—Is the omission of the (so-called) article justifiable? Note that the expression seems naturally to follow the historic present of the preceding sentence, though its employment appears harsh in conjunction with the past forms *was* and *were*. Compare "the spring before last," a little lower down.

The Psalmist's limit.—"The days of our years are three score years and ten."

Ten years more, &c.—One of the unsolved, insoluble problems of history is, what would have been the future of England if Cromwell had been spared for these "ten years more." Carlyle was evidently of the opinion that under his fostering care Puritanism would have triumphed ; but Puritanism had a fair chance in New England, and it did not triumph; in fact the robust character of the Briton is as little likely to adopt the extreme views of the Puritan as those of the Ritualist ; and the sturdy common sense of the nation, in the new world as well as in the old, has discarded many of the visionary projects so dear to the ardent supporters of the Protector in his own day and in ours. With all his intelligence, Carlyle seems not to have been able to free himself from the belief that events are predetermined, not merely, as Shakespeare puts it, that

> " There is a divinity that shapes our ends,
> Rough hew them how we will."

but that our ends are over-ruled by an inexorable destiny which leaves us not even the power to rough hew them ; and yet, notwithstanding this belief, he is eternally berating his fellowmen for not making the proper use of their free will. He is not, however, the only thinker who has reached absurdity while endeavoring to reconcile the irreconcilable doctrines of Freedom and Predestination.

Labor, of head and heart and hand.—Distinguish these labors. What figures of speech are employed?

The Manzinis, &c.—Do not confound *Manzini* with *Manzoni*, the author of *I Promessi Spoza*; nor with *Mazzini*, the friend of Kossuth, Ledru-Rollin, and Garibaldi. Manzini and the Duc de Créqui were ambassadors to the Court of the Protector, and their continental "splendors," in marked contrast with the sombre style of Hampton Court, were no doubt "interesting to the street population," etc. Note the contrasts in this paragraph and the one following.

Hampton Court—ten miles from London, celebrated in earlier times for the *conference* held there, contains a fine collection of Raphael's cartoons. Cardinal Wolsey and his royal master, the bluff King Henry VIII., erected the palace ; neither James I., nor Cromwell, the overthrower of his dynasty, did much to improve the place; but William of Orange, and his Dutch gardeners, made the grounds, the gardens, and the maze one of the great "sights" in the vicinity of the metropolis.

A private scene.—A metaphor taken from the stage. What is the relation of the word *there?*

The Lady Claypole.—Elizabeth, the second daughter and sixth child of the Protector, married her father's master of the horse, Claypole, one of the new House of Peers by which Cromwell so foolishly sought to give dignity to his legislation. The **weeping sisters** were Bridget, Mary, and Frances, the last of whom had, a few months previously, buried her husband, after only three short months of married life, so that she was still "in her weeds." Note the pathos of the remainder of this paragraph, and compare it with Thackeray's description of the madness of George III. The classical allusions (as to the "Pallida Mors" of the Latin poet, Horace), the Scriptural references and quotations, and the style of half soliloquy, and broken ejaculation show how complete a master Carlyle could be of the tender and pathetic in composition.

George Fox (1624-1690) was one of the most remarkable religious reformers the world has seen. Trained by a pious mother, he, at the age of nineteen, conceived that he had a divine commission to preach the doctrine of the sufficiency of conscience as a more certain guide than even the Scriptures.

A justice named Bennet, who, in conjunction with his fellow justices, committed Fox, at Derby, in 1650, on a false charge of blasphemy, gave his followers the nickname "Quakers," because the sturdy accused had called upon this ruler of the people to quake, or "tremble, at the name of the Lord." · The Quakers, or Friends, as they preferred to call themselves, objected to oaths, to baptism, to the Eucharist, to showing such marks of respect as uncovering the head in presence of superiors, to the use of plural forms in addressing single individuals, and to many other things equally harmless, so that it is not much wonder their founder, in spite of the general blamelessness of his life, found himself often in prison on account of his heterodox views. That Cromwell took his

part against the Puritan bigotry of the age speaks volumes both
for the purity of Fox and the liberality of the Protector. That
they should be persecuted by the dissolute and corrupt supporters
of the rule of Charles II. was inevitable; but it is impossible, in
the limits of a brief note, to do adequate justice to one of the most
remarkable religious reformers of an age prolific in men content to
sacrifice leisure, liberty, and life in attestation of their principles.

Hacker's men.—Col. Hacker was one of the most zealous
supporters of the Parliament in its long struggle against the arbitrary proceedings of the Crown, and no doubt he must have felt a
gloomy joy on being chosen, with two equally fanatical colonels,
to superintend the execution of the dethroned Charles. Hacker
was not, however, more inclined than his Puritan confrères to grant
the same religious and political toleration to others that they ex-
acted for themselves; and poor George Fox's arrest and first interview with the more tolerant Protector, were due to the fanatical
zeal of Hacker and his men.

Brought them to the Mews.—The place referred to here
was, in Cromwell's time, and subsequently, used as the Court
stables, situated in the vicinity of Charing Cross, London. Stow's
"Survey of London" informs us that a range of stables was built
here in the reigns of Edward VI., and Mary, on the site of what
had been "the Mewse, so-called of the King's falcons there kept
by the royal falconer—an office of great account," etc. Pennant
and Sir Walter Scott give the same account and origin of the word.
It originally meant, in English, a "cage for hawks," whence the
verb *mew* = to enclose; later the verb was used as an equivalent for
"to moult." or cast the feathers, and this is the original meaning
of the word in the French. *Muer* = Lat. *mutare* = to change, for
movitare, from *movere*, to move. The word *mews* is also applied
to ranges of outhouses in general.

Hampton-court park—was afterwards converted by William III. into the celebrated gardens and labyrinth.

"**Waft**" (*whiff*) "**of death.**"—Is *whiff* a fair equivalent
for *waft*? *Whiff* is an onomatopoetic word, meaning *puff* (cf. a
whiff of smoke); whereas *waft* properly means "a sign," or signal
given by *waving* a flag, or some similar object. A whiff of death
might emanate *from* a man doomed by illness; but does it not
seem more likely that the excited imagination of the enthusiast
saw and felt, by his "inner light," some *sign*, or "*waft*, of death go
forth *against* him." Note that Carlyle construes the word *against*
as meaning "to his disadvantage," a sense in which Fox certainly
did not intend it.

Nell Gwynn,—or *Gwynne*, as it is more commonly spelled,
having been a singer at taverns, an actress at the Court theatre,

and other things even worse, became the mistress of Charles II., over whom she exercised a powerful influence, and generally a good and patriotic influence. It is to her credit that she devoted the earnings of her life of shame to the meritorious work of founding and endowing Chelsea Hospital for the relief of worn-out soldiers. The dissolute companions of the "Merry Monarch" dubbed him the "Nell-Gwynne Defender," in derision of his kingly title of Defender of the Faith—a title first conferred by the Pope on Henry VIII., and still retained by the Sovereign. The association of Charles with "two centuries of all-victorious cant" is rather startling; he, indeed, had not even the grace to be guilty of hypocrisy, "the homage that vice renders to virtue."

My unfortunate George—probably alludes to the repeated imprisonments suffered by Fox for violation of the Conventicle Acts, directed against the practice of private non-conformist worship so dear to the Friends. There is besides a subtle contrast between the *fortunes* of the King and those of the persecuted Quaker; just as he scornfully contrasts the *merry* life of the former with that of the great Protector "looking to give it up," and with that of the Reformer at the beginning of his career "in the hollow of the tree" and "clad permanently in leather," as we learn from the record of his life.

To speak farther.—The *th* has crept improperly into this word by confounding it with *further*. *Farther* = *at* a greater distance, or length, is the irregular comparative of *far*, and should be written *farrer*—it is written *ferrer* in Piers Plowman; *further* = *to* a greater distance, is the regular comparative of *forth* = forward, in advance.

Harvey—was a zealous Puritan, who held the office of Groom of the Bedchamber to Cromwell, and has left us an account of his leader's last days, marked by the quaint simplicity, fervor, and disregard of grammar of the period. There was another and more celebrated Harvey, the discoverer of the circulation of the blood, who had held the post of Court Physician to James I., and Charles I., and had died in 1657, the year before the death of the Protector.

Ever worsening = constantly growing worse—the correct meaning—A.S. *wyrsian*. Milton uses *worsen* transitively = to make worse. It is a pity that an expressive word like this should be permitted to die; it still occurs (intransitively) as a provincialism, and has been used by Gladstone and others in imitation of Carlyle.

"Bastard tertian" = a spurious, not genuine, tertian. There are three kinds of intermittent fever,—*quotidian*, in which the attacks occur every 24 hours, in the morning; *tertian*, at intervals of 48 hours, at midday; and *quartan*, every 72 hours, in the evening. *Bastard* is derived from *bastum* = a pack-saddle, with the common suffix, *ard* (cf. cow*ard*, dot*ard*). *Ague,* old French *ague* — *aigu,* Lat. *acuta.*

Strongly laying hold on God.—The familiar fervor of some of the Puritan writers sounds occasionally almost like blasphemy to our modern ears. Carlyle entered deeply into the spirit of these "Old English Worthies," and to him there seemed no irreverence in the "authentic wrestlings of ancient Human Souls," —wrestlings as of Jacob with the Angel. The extravagance of romance has caricatured the fervent piety of the Puritans, representing them as fanatical and illiterate. But the writings of such men as "Owen, Goodwin, Sterry," Calamy, and Baxter abundantly disprove the charge.

Owen, Rev. John, was born in 1616, matriculated at Queen's College, Oxford, at the very early age of twelve, wrote learnedly and voluminously on many subjects of controversy, enjoyed the confidence and friendship of Fairfax and Cromwell, was chosen to preach before Parliament the day after the execution of Charles I., —a sermon in which he never once alluded to that dread event— and lived to thank Charles II. for his Declaration of Indulgence. He died in 1683.

Goodwin, Rev. Thomas, was born in 1600, and matriculated shortly before reaching his thirteenth birthday, at Christ Church, Cambridge. He, too, was an able controversialist and preacher. Died 1679.

Authentic wrestlings.—When applied to a literary production there is a decided difference in meaning between *authentic* and *genuine;* but in spite of Trench's efforts to draw a sharp line between them, these words continue to be used as synonyms in other applications.—*Authentic* = αὐθεντικός, αὐθέντης; the first syllable is unquestionably the same as in αὐτός = self, but can the aspirate θ be accounted for on the supposition that the second syllable is ἑντ = sant = asant, a present participle of *as* = to be, seeing that neither *ens* in Lat., nor ὤν in Gk. was aspirated,—and further that *asant* would naturally become *a(s)ant* = *ant*, dropping the *s* between two vowels in accordance with a well-known law? May it not be ἑντ, the stem of ἵημι = send forth, which would make αὐθέντης = one who sends forth his own work?

Transcendent.—Note that Carlyle italicises the word, thus showing that he uses it in the technical sense in which it is used in philosophy, viz., going beyond the limits of empiricism, or experience; their "wishes" went beyond what their experience showed to be possible, and so they were "hoping to prevail with the Inexorable."

A great scene—the exit—metaphors taken from the stage, cf. Shakespeare's "All the world's a stage," etc. "They have their *exits,*" etc,

He died—as the Brave have all done.—In illustration of this truth take the death of Nelson as described by his officers ; and the death of Charles I., in front of this same palace of Whitehall, where the Protector now lay at rest.

Thurloe—was private secretary to the Protector, and it is somewhat strange that he should not have known of the existence of the "sealed paper." The welcome accorded to Charles II., the fact that his most inglorious reign was allowed to close in comparative peace, and the indulgence granted by his subjects to the vices of their "Merry Monarch" seemed to show such a rooted antipathy to the stringent rule of Puritanism that it appears to be at least doubtful whether the question of appointing Oliver's successor was the "matter of much moment," etc., that Carlyle believed it to be. The truth is that the people of England were sick for a change, and neither Fleetwood nor Richard Cromwell could have long prevented it.

Dunbar and Worcester.—Where were these places? Describe the Victories.

To-morrow is September Third.—Note the faulty construction. If this is the historic present tense, the same tense should have been used throughout the paragraph.

Annihilating and judging himself—counting himself as nothing, Lat. *ad nihil.*

Consternation and astonishment = a feeling of being overwhelmed and astounded, or stunned: Lat. *con, sterno* = to overwhelm; in *astonish* the *ish* is of recent origin, the older form being *astony*, cf. Milton's "astonied stood," A.S. *astunian* = to stun completely,—cf. French *étonner*, Low-Lat. *extonare.*

Husht, poor weeping Mary !—hush! husht! hist! whist! and the Hibernicism whisht! are all imitative words having the same meaning of enforcing silence. Mary was the Protector's third daughter, and was married to Lord Fauconberg.

Cromwell's works have done and are still doing ! —It looks as though the wish were father to this thought, and that Carlyle is himself only too conscious that his hero's works have *not* done *all* that might be desired or even expected of them; for our author immediately plunges into an hysterical shriek of scolding that increases in virulence to the end. That the Protector's mark has been impressed on the centuries is unquestionably true; but it is hardly less true that Shakespeare's aphorism holds good of Cromwell as of other men :—

> " The evil that men do lives after them ;
> The good is oft interred with their bones."

Explain the allusions in " Revolutions of eighty-eight;" " tyrannous Star Chambers;" " England's Puritanism—soon goes." Note the intensity of Carlyle's hatred of the Established Church, and the bad taste with which he assails forms of worship that, whether they be right or wrong, are, nevertheless, held in respect by millions of his fellowmen. Force is his demigod and is one of his attributes ; of politeness he hardly understood the meaning.

Men's ears are not now slit off, &c.—probably in allusion, specially, to the punishment inflicted on Prynne, author of the *Histriomastix.*

Owl—A. S. *úle;* cf. Lat. *ulula,* and Sanskrit *uluka*—cf. also *Howl.*

Two centuries of Hypocrisis—explained in the parenthesis immediately following. Cf. "Two centuries of Cant." The play on these words is certainly not so vulgar and coarse as his play on the words "*à posteriori,*" "*other* extremity." Explain the meaning of the logical terms "*a priori*" and "*a posteriori.*"

WILLIAM MAKEPEACE THACKERAY.—1811–1863.

The Reconciliation.—*From* Henry Esmond.—Extract LXIII., page 308.

Biographical Sketch.—Names are sometimes misnomers, and this was to some extent true of William Makepeace Thackeray, for he considered it his duty, and it certainly was his pleasure, to *make war* on the shams, foibles, and follies of the Englishman of the nineteenth century. He was born in Calcutta, in 1811, where his father, a civil servant of the then existing East India Company, was accumulating an ample fortune, which he shortly afterwards bequeathed to his little son. It has ever been the custom of the Anglo-Indians to send their children home to the "old country" in order to guard them against the effects of the fatal climate of Hindüstan ; and accordingly the child was sent home while yet little more than an infant. He was educated at the Charterhouse (a school that has produced many of the most brilliant contributors to English literature) ; and at the usual age he matriculated at Trinity College, Cambridge. He did not, however, graduate at the University ; and though we know little more of his college career than the fact that he occasionally wrote for his University organ, *The Snob*, we may not unfairly conclude from his confessions in the breezy pages of his *Adventures of Philip* that he belonged to the extravagant coterie, and spent his money as easily as it had come to him. At all events he seems to have found the Cambridge atmosphere either uncongenial or expensive ; for he left it to make the grand tour of the Continent, considered at that time even more necessary than a college course for the completion of a polite education. On his travels his money went as fast as at Cambridge, and shortly after his setting out we find him endeavoring to retrieve his lost patrimony by turning his natural talents to account. At first he tried drawing and painting, for which he had some talent but no genius ; but having failed, in 1835, as Dickens tells us, to obtain the position of artistic illustrator of the *Pickwick Papers*, he determined to emulate the example of their author, and henceforth he devoted himself almost exclusively to literature.

For many years after their first meeting in 1835, Thackeray and Dickens held the first places, if they did not appropriate the honors, in the ranks of English novelists ; and it is greatly to the credit of the former that he on all occasions willingly acknowledged the superiority of his great rival in the delineation of such characters as appealed most forcibly to the feelings of the people. Dickens was, in iced, the missionary of the lower and lower-middle

classes, interpreting their feelings, their wishes, their hopes and
their aspirations as no novelist had ever done before him ; but
Thackeray was no less the exponent of the characteristic peculiarities of the upper and upper-middle classes, their prejudices,
their fears, their mode of life, and their modes of thought. Endowed by nature with a keen insight into the intricacies of the
human mind, and educated by experience into a due appreciation
of the general hollowness of Society, he was well qualified to
become the satirist and censor of his age ; and it must be acknowledged that he has in general tried to discharge his satirical
function fairly, though his keen sense of humor and his conse-
quent tendency to indulge in burlesque have frequently betrayed
him into exaggerations that are neither merciful nor just. In his
Memoirs of Barry Lyndon, for example, he has given a type of
the mere fortune-hunting, or rather *heiress*-hunting, Irishman of
the playwrights—a character as untrue to life as is the ordinary
comic Irishman of the ordinary Irish farce ; it is, in fact, the caricature of an exaggerated caricature. He knew nothing, and he
did not seem to care to know anything, of the characters of those
not born within the sphere or within the influence of the Upper
Ten. But within this limited area he knew everything : he is
equally happy in depicting the generous, choleric, simple-minded
Colonel Newcome ; the frank, foolish, stout-hearted Philip ; and
the humorous pomposity of the servants' hall. The gorgeous
romances of Disraëli are utterly misleading as to the tastes and
habits of the aristocracy, because he painted them as he imagined
they *ought* to be ; but Thackeray's keen sense of humor protected
him from such an error, and he has painted them as they are,—
or, at least, as he believed them to be.

He did not spring into notoriety ; on the contrary, he had been
for years a constant contributor to *The Times*, to *Fraser's Magazine*,
and other periodicals and papers, under (or over) the *noms de plume*
of Michael Angelo Titmarsh, George Fitznoodle, Esq., Charles
J. Yellowplush, &c., before the public recognized him as one of
our great humorists and satirists. But though he rose slowly he
rose steadily in the estimation of the reading public, till it became
a subject of controversy whether Dickens depicted the humors of
low life, or Thackeray the follies of high life with the greater
truthfulness.—In 1851 he delivered a course of lectures (frequently repeated) on *The English Humorists of the Eighteenth
Century*, and afterwards a series on *The Four Georges*, from
which he derived not only pecuniary advantage as a direct result,
but no slight addition to his growing reputation as a singularly
clear, judicious, and withal kindly critic of his fellow-craftsmen in
the literary world. In addition to more sustained efforts he, as

"Our Fat Contributor," wrote many fugitive sketches, witty and humorous, for the pages of *Punch* from its foundation in 1841 ; and his *Roundabout Papers* in the *Cornhill Magazine*, of which he was editor for many years, used to be looked for with an avidity only to be compared to the eagerness of the public for the appearance of the *Spectator* in the days of Addison. He joined the legal profession and was called to the bar in 1848,—probably in deference to his own opinion that every man ought to have a profession, and in some distrust as to whether Literature gave him the right to say that he already had a profession ; but the question was decided by the success of his *Vanity Fair* (1847–1848), the publication of which greatly enhanced the reputation already gained by his *Paris Sketch-Book*, his *Irish Sketch-Book*, and his *Cornhill to Cairo*. His later publications followed as rapidly as could be expected from one with his *dolce-far-niente* proclivities ; but it will always be a disputable point whether any of these, and if any, which of them, has added to the fame conferred upon him by *Vanity Fair*. He was by no means a great original thinker, nor was he gifted with the dramatic power requisite for the construction of a carefully devised plot, and the natural indolence of his Anglo-Indian origin and early exemption from the necessity to work always prevented him from making any great exercise of inventive genius. His indolence also left his work more slipshod and unpolished than that of any other great writer of his day ; and many of even his finest passages are marred by a carelessness that may be fairly called slovenly. Nor is there one of his plots that does not fairly lie open to the same charge ; the stories are vapid and uninteresting, the incidents have no natural sequence, and it makes little difference at what page one begins or ceases to read. In the delineation of character, however (within the range already indicated), he stands unrivalled; his characters, it is true, are not always originals,—one may without difficulty recognize the features of *Sir Roger de Coverley* and others of the portrait-gallery of the older humorists in Thackeray's heroes ; but the copy is in many cases a much better picture than the original. The earlier humorists painted in bolder, coarser colors, but Thackeray gave a more subtle touch to the portrait : there is, for example, nothing in the work of these early humorists so fine as that scene in which the unprincipled adventuress, *Becky Sharp*, is represented as exulting in the victory of her outraged husband over the graceless scamp for whom she had deserted him—an unconscious touch of nature that first suggested to the author the idea that he really had the genius of a novelist. *Pendennis, Henry Esmond*, with its sequel *The Virginians*, and *The Newcomes* share the first honors with their precursor, *Vanity Fair*,

and it is doubtful to which of these should be awarded the palm
of merit ; they have, each and all, the same defects and the same
excellences, a carelessness of composition and plot in marked contrast with an admirably careful portrayal of character. Besides
these works and the others already mentioned Thackeray wrote
several burlesques and satirical sketches in prose as well as a considerable number of humorous ballads and short poems in imitation
of the *Odes* of Horace and the lyrics of Béranger. In his *Peg of
Limavaddy* and other Irish ballads he has pretty well imitated
the jingle of the old Irish "lilt," and their language is a fair
enough imitation of the "brogue" to deceive the average English
reader—but they have neither the sweet music, the metaphorical
language, nor the introspective subtlety of the original ballad ;
while their flippancy is in marked contrast with the depth of
passionate feeling pervading alike all Irish music and all Irish
song. In 1855-1856 he visited America, where he delivered his
series of lectures with marked success. On his return to England
he made an unsuccessful attempt to get into Parliament, in 1857,
and thenceforward devoted himself exclusively to literary pursuits.
On the morning before Christmas, 1863, he was found dead in his
bed,—his death being even more sudden and unexpected than
that of his great rival, Dickens.

THE RECONCILIATION.

The extract is one of the finest passages in what some consider
to be the author's finest production ; and it illustrates as fairly as
could be done in a mere extract some of Thackeray's peculiar
excellences and special faults. The narrator is supposed to be
Esmond himself, but if we compare Esmond's reflections and
general modes of thought with those of Thackeray in his Lectures
on the Humorists we can easily see that the hero is in truth a
gentleman of the nineteenth century relegated to the reign of
Queen Anne. The author has, it is true, caught the "manner of
speech" of his predecessors with remarkable exactness, and his
sense of humor was too keen to admit of his committing any
serious mistake in this respect ; but he was at once too indolent
and too undramatic to represent the characteristic features of a
bygone age with more than a superficial accuracy. His power of
discriminating character and portraying it by subtle touches was
wonderful, but it was the power of portraying such characters as
he had met with ; hence his very best creations are rather repro-
ductions than originals, and they present such complex features
as might be expected in characters depicted partly from observa-

tion of his contemporaries and partly from historical study. *Lady Castlewood* is a singularly sweet and pure type of womanhood, but a very slight change in her mode of dress and speech would render her the well-bred gentlewoman of any age ; *Frank* would stand as a type of the manly, impulsive, high-souled boy, whether wearing an Eton collar or *point de Venise;* and one has nowhere to seek very far for a *Mr. Tusher*, with "an authoritative voice," though without "a great black periwig." Read carefully the introductory foot-note to the extract in the Reader.

Cathedral—Lat. and Gk. *Cathedra* = a chair, is the principal church within the diocese, or jurisdiction of a bishop, and is so named because he has his chair or throne there. Winchester Cathedral alluded to here was one of the eight Cathedrals of the New Foundation re-established by Henry VIII. on the overthrow of the monasteries formerly attached to them.

Dean and some of his clergy—*Dean* was originally = one set over *ten* monks, Lat. *decanus, decem;* the dean and clergy of the Cathedral constituted "the chapter," and gradually usurped to themselves the power over the Cathedral originally vested in the bishop.

Choristers, young and old—forming a separate corporation of "lay vicars" in many of the Cathedrals, and maintained from funds derived from special estates provided for this purpose by the decent piety of a past age.

Beside the dean—Which is *beside* or *besides* the proper word in this connection ? *See* Ayer.

Read from the eagle in—voice and—periwig—The eagle was then and still continues to be a favorite design for the *lectern*, or reading-desk, in the better class of Anglican churches. Note the effect of the zeugma ; this figure is frequently used, as here, for the purpose of introducing a witty juxtaposition of un-expected incongruities. It is at best but a low species of wit, the frequent occurrence of which would be intolerable. *Periwig* is a mis-spelt form of *periwig* = Dutch *peruyk :* the erroneous opinion that *peri* was a prefix led to its being dropped, whence *wig*. *Peruke* comes from Fr. *perruque*, a word of the same origin as the other.

Point de Venise—Venetian lace has been superseded by French and English products.

Vandyke—or better Vandyck, Sir Anthony, one of the most eminent of portrait-painters, was born at Antwerp, 1599, and died in London, 1641. His first master, VanBalen, had studied in Italy, where he himself subsequently became the disciple of Rubens, surpassing even his great master in the nearness of his approach to the delicate flesh-tints of their common ideal of perfection,

Titian. This early training accounts for the utter absence of Flemish influence from his works—the greatest of which, "The Crucifixion," pronounced by Sir Joshua Reynolds to be "one of the finest pictures in the world," is as truly Italian as any of the works of Titian. He was knighted and pensioned by Charles I., whose favor enabled the artist to realize a handsome fortune as the most popular portrait-painter of his age.

Mons. Rigaud's portrait, &c.—This portrait is several times alluded to. *Rigaud* appears to have been the popular portrait-painter of the day at Paris.

Not much chance—no small tenderness—What figure of speech ?

Anthem—This word has no connection with the root of τίθημι; it is a doublet of *antiphon*, a later introduction of the same meaning—a psalm *sung responsively* by the choir, which was divided into two parts, as it still is in Cathedrals and College Chapels ; from A. S. *antefn*, which is a mere abbreviation of ἀντίφωνα, ἀντί and φωνή.

Melancholy—The old physicians attributed this mental condition to the presence of *black bile*, μέλας χολή. Were they, after all, so very far astray ? A similar idea has given us *humor*, *distemper*, and other words of like character.

As that dear lady beheld him—*Lady*, A. S. *hlǽfdige*, is certainly derived from *hláf = loaf*, as to its first syllable, and probably from A. S. *díg = a kneaded lump, dough*, as to the second syllable,—so that its original meaning == *loaf-kneader*. So the word *lord*, A. S. *hláford*, is certainly from *hláf*, and probably from *weard = keeper* (cf. *warden*), the meaning being *loaf-keeper*, or master.

The inner chapel—the portion of the church adjacent to the altar. The Lat. *capella* was originally used to indicate the shrine in which was preserved the *cappa* (cope) of St. Martin, and subsequently for any sanctuary.

Before the clergy were fairly gone—This phrase shows the boy's extreme eagerness, it being considered a rude violation of propriety for any of the congregation to leave their seats till the officiating clergy had retired. Note also how this eagerness is shown by the jumble of moods and tenses in Frank's salutation.

The quarrel was all over.—In this passage note particularly the effect of the climax, immediately followed by the amplified anti-climax—"sister, mother, goddess"—but goddess no more, "for he knew of her weaknesses;" mother no more, for "by thought, suffering, experience, he was older *now* than she;" sister no more, for now she was "more fondly cherished as *woman*," and they no longer cared to look upon each other as mere brother and sister. No man could write ·more purely, sweetly, and tenderly than Thackeray when the mood was on him ; pity that his indolence so constantly stood in the way of his exertions!

So that he might see again once more.—Criticise this sentence. Is it really tautological ? Explain " so that."

Bid Beatrix put her ribbons on, &c.—Ribbons were not so common that even Beatrice could wear them constantly. The word is the Celtic *ribin*, and has no connection with *band;* hence the present spelling is preferable to *riband* or *ribband*. *Maid of honor*—one of the young ladies who wait upon the Queen, as companions and attendants, not as ¦menials. *Fine set-up minx*— *fine* refers to the dress or finery, old French *fin*, Lat. *finitus; set-up* is intended to describe the manners, cf. stuck-up ; *minx*, a term of endearment = little dear,—a contracted, and possibly plural, form of *minikin*, from the German *minne* = love;—the word is sometimes used in a bad sense, though not implying much beyond a mild, playful censure.

Heart was never in the church—*i.e.*, in the profession; κυριακόν = Lord's house, κύριος = Lord, A. S. *cyrice*. Cf. *kirk*.

Asunder = on sunder, which form occurs in the Bible; A.S. *onsundran*.

Must try the world first before he tires of it—the wisdom here is better than the grammar—criticise the sentence.

Chaplain—from *chapel;* the Low Lat. *capella* originally meant " the sanctuary in which was preserved the *cope* of St. Martin,"—Low Lat. *capa, cappa*, cf. *cap, cape*.

Young Lord Churchill—son and successor to the great Duke of Marlborough. Write a brief note on the careers of Marlborough and Lady Marlborough.

Dowager lady, your father's widow—*dowager* = a widow having a jointure; from Fr. *douer*, Lat. *dotare* = to endow, comes the coined word *dowage* = endowment, and from this latter the coined word *dowager*. Thackeray employs the word as it is now commonly used, to distinguish the *widow* of the former from the *wife* of the present holder of the title and estate; the word is also sometimes used (improperly) to denote an elderly woman without any reference to jointure, title, or estates. Why does Lady Castlewood, speaking to Esmond, call her " your father's widow?" *See* int. foot-note in High School Reader, page 308.

Esmond said, " Yes, as far as present favor went,"&c. —an instance of our author's negligence—Esmond's words being partly in oblique and partly in direct narrative. Re-write the speech, first in direct narrative, and then in oblique.

Frantic = out of one's senses, full of madness. The older forms were *frentik* and *frenetik*, Gr. φρενητιχος, suffering from φρενιτις, φρήν = the mind.

Mr. Atterbury of St. Bride's—1662-1732—became successively chaplain to Queen Anne, dean of Carlisle, and bishop of Rochester. He was an eloquent preacher, an able writer, and a zealous leader of the High Church party of his day (differing very widely from the High Church party of to-day); he was, besides, an active politician of the Jacobite party, and entered heart and soul into the conspiracy for the restoration of the direct Stuart line by placing the Pretender on the throne at the death of Anne. For this he was tried and convicted by the House of Lords in 1723, deprived of his See, and sentenced to banishment, which he spent mainly in Paris till his death nine years afterwards.

"**You had spared, &c.**"—Parse each word in this sentence.

Such humility, as made—*Such*. A. S. *Swyle* = so like, the *l* being lost. The word *as* is a true relative; it was formerly common, though now found as a provincialism only, except after the words *such* and *same*, in which positions this form of the relative still holds its place in good English.—It is a corruption of the Scand. rel. pron. *es* = *which*, and must not be confounded with the entirely different word *as*, the adverb and conjunction, which is a corruption of *also*, A. S. *eal swá* = just so, just as, the *l* being lost by a corruption similar to what we have seen in the word *such*.

I own that—Explain the meaning of *own*. What other meaning has it ?

I knew you would come—and saw, &c.—the emotional confusion of the agitated lady is well exhibited by the ungrammatical language, the incoherence of the thoughts, the importance attached to trifling coincidences, the reiteration of the words of the anthem which still ring in her ears like the refrain of some heart-reaching song, and finally by the hysterical outburst of happy laughter and tears in which all memory of that sad year of loneliness and estrangement was washed away for ever.

The concluding paragraph is worthy of Thackeray at his best ; it scarce contains a word (except, perhaps, the 'quite' in *l*. 5) that could be altered or omitted without marring the melody and beauty of the whole.

"**Non omnis moriar !**"=—"I shall not wholly die." The quotation is from the well known ode "Exegi monumentum ære perennius," with which Horace closes the third book of the Odes, intending thenceforth to abandon lyric poetry ; the full quotation is

Non omnis moriar ! Multaque pars mei
Vitabit Libitinam.   Odes, III. 30.

Horace bases his hopes of escaping the oblivion of the tomb on his success as a lyric poet ; write a short essay contrasting this with the basis of the same hope given in the text.

HENRY WADSWORTH LONGFELLOW.—1807–1882.

The Hanging of the Crane.—Extract LXVII., page 336.

Biographical sketch.—Henry Wadsworth Longfellow, born February 27, 1807, was the son of Stephen Longfellow, a distinguished lawyer and United States Congressman, and his wife, Zilpha, whose family name of Wadsworth is preserved in that of her gifted son. At the age of fourteen he entered Bowdoin College, about twenty-five miles from Portland; and graduated in 1825, at an age when the majority of boys are thinking about matriculating. Among his classmates was Nathaniel Hawthorne, not much less distinguished in prose than Longfellow subsequently became in poetry. Shortly after leaving college he was offered the professorship of modern languages by the authorities; and in order to qualify himself for the position he spent nearly four years in travel and study on the continent of Europe. What would have been his influence on American literature, and especially on American poetry, had he not spent these years in Europe, it would be idle to conjecture; he was not fitted to be the poet of a turbulent democracy, either by taste, temperament, physique, or predilection; and though he conformed with a peculiar sweetness and urbanity to the exactions of his admiring countrymen, one can easily see that it was with a very positive feeling of relief he escaped to the seclusion of his study to hold sweet communion with the semi-æsthetic mediæval catholicity imbibed during his European tours. He left America, a callow poet with a certain abstract love for nature as he had seen her on Casco Bay, and with a certain power, not fully recognized even by himself, of interpreting her, as she is, apart from the supernatural; he returned, in 1829, to assume his position in Bowdoin College, steeped to the lips in the mediæval traditions of the monks and brotherhoods, and no longer able to discern Nature, face to face, but only dimly seeing her in the light reflected from the convent walls and walks, and hearing her as she rustles in dim, ghost-like legendary guise through the marble corridors of the cloister. He had been among the lotus eaters, and their mysticism and music had so entranced him that not for many years did he emerge, nor did he ever fully awake to the fact that he lived in the most active age and was, in name at least, a citizen among the most active people the world has yet beheld.

During the six years (1829–1835) spent at Bowdoin College he published an essay on the *Moral and Devotional Poetry of Spain*, which included some excellent translations from the Spanish poets, and *Outre-Mer* (*Ultra Mare*), a record of impressions and incidents

of his travels ; but though the prose of these productions is marked
by a peculiar gracefulness, there is nothing in the poetry to show
any power beyond that of correctly interpreting the thoughts of
others, nothing so original or powerful as the *Burial of the Minne-
sink*, written during his undergraduate novitiate to the Muses.

In 1835, he was elected to the chair of Modern Languages and
Belles-lettres in Harvard College, Cambridge, near Boston : and to
better qualify himself for the position, he once more visited Europe,
spending some fifteen months in the study of the Scandinavian
literature, and in contemplation of the sublime scenery of Switzerland. On his return to America, in 1836, he settled amid the
congenial surroundings of Cambridge, where he purchased the old
frame house formerly occupied as headquarters by Washington
during the Revolutionary War. Here he continued to reside till
the time of his death, only breaking the monotony of an unevent-
ful life by occasional visits to Europe, and by periodical trips to
his summer residence at Nahant, and to the residences of his children at Castine and at Portland.

It would occupy too much space to criticise his works in detail—
even to give a catalogue of them would go beyond the limits of this
brief sketch ; but it is not necessary, for many of his poems—all,
probably, that will survive—are to his admirers " familiar in their
mouths as household words," and familiar they will continue to be
long after the works of abler men have passed away into forgetfulness. And why? Because of all the men that have lived in our
day, Longfellow was the one man that threw open his inmost heart
of hearts to all his fellows; because that, having nothing to conceal,
his life, his character, his works were unreservedly displayed to the
gaze of the world, and the world could see that his conduct was in
all things conformed to his creed : and because that in this high-
pressure, working, struggling, thinking, doubting age, he has
taught us, in language that even a child can understand, to pause
and look, for

> Nature with folded hands seemed there !
> Kneeling at her evening prayer !

not, perhaps, a very lofty conception of Nature in these days when
natural laws are the be-all and the end-all of the wise : but it
is at least a conception of Nature which has touched the great
heart of the people, and the lessons of the *Songs of Evening*—the
" Psalm of Life," the " Excelsior," the " Resignation," and the
rest of them—will be read, and learned, and loved by generations
yet unborn, long after the æsthetic materialism of the age shall
have become the bye-word, the reproach, and the laughing-stock
of a more enlightened future.

That many of his shorter poems will live seems as certain as that any of our present literature will survive; but it is more doubtful whether a similar destiny awaits any of his more elaborate effusions. *Evangeline, The Courtship of Miles Standish, Hiawatha*, and *The Golden Legend*, will probably be found, in libraries at least, for many years to come ; but whether they will become a permanent part of the living literature of the language is not so easy to decide. *Hiawatha* is unique, there is nothing like it in the language, and even were it destitute of other merit (which it is not), this should be sufficient to ensure its immortality ; *Evangeline* ought to survive on account of the singular beauty of her character and the sweet, sad story of her married career; but it does not seem likely that *Miles Standish* will long outlive the obliteration of the old New England landmarks of prejudice and Puritanism; and the *Golden Legend* will probably be unread till some new upheaval of society restores once more the departing taste for mediævalism.

Longfellow was twice married. In 1831, being then in his twenty-fourth year, he married Miss Mary Potter, who died at Rotterdam, 1835, while accompanying her husband on his tour of preparation for his duties at Harvard ; she was the " Being Beauteous" of whom he speaks in " Footsteps of Angels " as one

" Who unto my youth was given,
More than all things else to love me,
And is now a saint in heaven."

Eight years afterwards, 1843, he married Miss Appleton, of Boston, who became the mother of his five children, Ernest, and Charles, and

" Grave Alice, and laughing Allegra,
And Edith with golden hair."

Her dress accidentally took fire, and she was burned to death, in their happy home in Cambridge, in 1861. He could bear to write of his first wife in the *Voices of the Night*, but he never could trust himself, in any published work, even to allude to the awfully tragic fate of her whose untimely death he mourned so patiently, so deeply, and so long.

THE HANGING OF THE CRANE.

This poem was first published in 1874, and reappeared the following year among the ' other poems' in *The Mask of Pandora, and other poems*. It was received cordially, as all the author's works were at this period, for his reputation had already been established on so secure a foundation that during a visit to Eng-

land a short time previously (1868-69), he had received the hono-
rary degrees of LL.D. from Cambridge, and D.C.L. from Oxford,
and had the year previous to its publication, been elected a member of the Russian Academy of Science, 1875. The style is characteristic of Longfellow, nor is the fable (or plot) less so, exhibiting as it does that intimate commingling of the real with the unreal,
of the actual with the visionary, which pervades all his poetry. In
his later years he became even more attached to this ghostly union
of the seen and the unseen, and the very form of the present extract reappears in his *Keramos*, 1878; though in the latter poem
the distinction between the scene of real life and the visionary
world of the poet is marked much more clearly and distinctly, the
preludes being purely descriptive of what passed before his bodily
eyes while the imaginative *corollaries* are distinctly visionary,
though not less real nor less effective. In the present poem the
preludes, it will be noticed, are scarcely, if at all, less visionary
than the imaginative scenes that follow them. It may also be
noticed that the poet, now no longer young, cannot bring himself
to depict the solitary state of one left there alone—"I see the two
alone remain." And this is characteristic of him,—he saw that the
upheaval of American society, brought about by the civil war,
boded disaster to the commonwealth, and that it was of the utmost
consequence that the people should be lured back to the joys of
domestic life; hence his pen pictures of the peace and joy of wedded bliss must not be marred by the blurs that had blotted out the
great happiness of his own fireside scene. Indeed, it was not in
the nature of this man, kindly, cheery, hopeful as it always was, to
give pain to any; and so we find in this, as in all his works, the
healing balm of consolation and of hope applied to soothe and cure
the wounds of separation and distress.

The title of the poem is taken from a custom of his New England home, where old-time customs are even now observed with a
fidelity unknown in other parts of the bustling, go-ahead Union.
On the old-time open hearths of New England used to blaze the
crackling logs, unhampered and unhidden by the burnished stove
that so greatly offended the æsthetic eye of Oscar Wilde; and on
this hearth the mode of cookery was, and still is in some places, as
primitive as it used to be before the Mayflower landed her living
freight on Plymouth Rock. An upright iron bar is secured in
sockets in which it can turn freely, and from near the top of this
bar projects an horizontal shaft of metal, from which are suspended
chains, hooks, cleets, and all the other contrivances for holding the
pots and kettles over the blazing logs below. This combination is
called the 'crane,' and the "Hanging of the Crane" is therefore
symbolical of the completion of the house for the reception of a

newly-wedded pair—it is, in fact, the New England equivalent for the silly "house-warming" of more advanced, but less homely and less happy places. The word is derived from the bird, the crane, cf. Gk. γέρανος, root *gar* = to croak.

I. Scan the opening prelude (1st six lines) ; name the metres ; and state the order of recurrence of the rhymes.

Guest—A. S. *gæst*, Lat. *hostis*, the primary meaning being an 'enemy,' then a 'stranger,' and finally a 'guest'—the *u* is inserted to keep the *g* hard. Sometimes derived from *hospitem* = host, but this is from *hosti-pet*, i.e. *hostis, potens,* = guest—master.

Jest—originally gesto = a tale, a merry tale, Lat. *gestum.*

Into the night are gone—distinguish between '*are* gone' and '*have* gone.'

Myriad—Gk. μυριάς = ten thousand, an immense number.

Like a new star, &c.—the discovery of stars unobserved before is not so uncommon as to make it necessary for us to suppose the poet to have had in mind any special theory as to the origin of the worlds. Longfellow was not a deep natural philosopher, and it is not at all likely that he had any intention of lending his poetic support to any hypothesis ; he wanted a suitable image, and he found an appropriate one in the idea of a new star "roll'd on its harmonious way." *Harmonious* is characteristic of Longfellow, who was ever hearing the deep symphonies of nature, as in some vast cathedral of the spheres.

Chimney, burning bright.—Is this an instance of *hypallage ?* or is it a transferred epithet ? What is the difference ? *Chimney,* Lat. *caminus,* Gk. κάμινος = oven, furnace, chimney,

II. **Muse on what, &c.**—the word has no connection with the nine Muses; it is derived from French, *muser* = to study, old Fr. *muse* = mouth, Italian *musare* = "to hold the muzzle, or snout, in the air,"—the image being obviously taken from the attitude of a dog, or other hunting animal, sniffing the air in doubt as to the proper course to follow. Cf. *muzzle*, which is simply the diminutive of Fr. *muse.* Note the graceful uncertainty, and the graceful expression of it, throughout this prelude.

For two alone—*all one* = quite by oneself; the word *one* was originally pronounced *own*, as in this word, and in *atone* = 'at one' ; it should properly be used with reference to a single object only; but Longfellow, and not he alone, confounds it with *lone*, *lonely* (with which it has no connection whatever), and so employs it incorrectly to agree with a plural, as in the present poem.

Light of love—cf. Gray's "bloom of young desire, and purple light of love."

Of love, that says not, &c.—The unselfishness and the soul-union of conjugal love are beautifully expressed in this couplet,—the love that puts not itself first, " *not mine* and thine," but looks upon both as one, recognizes no divided interest, is willing even to sink itself to the second place in the spirit of self-sacrifice, " *ours,* for ours is *thine* and mine." The remainder of the stanza, too, shows very prettily the completeness of the contentment in each other's society ; they want no guests to check, as a screen might do, the natural impulse to cast tender glances, and to worry them with dull, prosy news of the dull, prosy world beyond their paradise of peace.

Tell them tales—' relate stories to them.' In Milton's " every shepherd *tells* his *tale* " the words have a very different meaning, viz., ' *counts* his *number*'— with which cf. the Biblical ' *tale* of bricks,' and the ' teller ' in a bank. This is an excellent example of the changes constantly occurring in the uses of words in all living languages

Needs must be —*needs* —of necessity, an adverb, old genitive *nedes,* which supplanted the still older genitive *nede,* A.S. *nyde,* gen. of *nyd.* Parse *each, other's, own.*

III. **Views, dissolving, &c.**—In allusion to the dissolving views of a magic lantern. **Transfigured** = with the figures changed.

Fancy—a contraction from *fantasy,* Gk. φαντασία, φαντάζω, φαίνω.

Self-same scene—The use of the word *self-same* is very unhappy, and is unlike the author's usual carefulness in the selection of terms : *self-same* is a compound of two purely Anglo-Saxon words, *self,* and *same,* differing very little from each other in meaning, and equivalent to " the very identical thing (or person) ;"—it should not, therefore, be applied to a scene, even " in part transfigured."

They entertain A little angel unaware—A love of children was a marked feature in the character of the poet, as, indeed, it is in the characters of all morally healthy men ; elsewhere (in the *Children*) he shows his love for them :—

" Oh ! what would the world be to us, If the children were no more ?
We should dread the desert behind us Worse than the dark before."

The sentiment in the text is most likely inspired by the apostolic injunction to the Hebrews (xiii. 2), " to entertain strangers : for thereby some have entertained angels unawares," in which the allusion is, of course, to the entertaining of angels by Abraham and by Lot. It is not strictly true to nature to describe parents as "unaware" of the *angelic* character of their first-born ; though the poets, no doubt carried away by the Biblical " unawares," persistently do so : for instance, Gerald Massey, in the *Ballad of Babe Cristabel,* has

> "In this dim world of clouding cares,
> We rarely know, till 'wildered eyes
> See white wings lessening up the skies,
> The Angels with us unawares."

And another poet, Charles M. Dickinson, says of them

> "They are idols of hearts and of households,
> They are Angels of God in disguise."

Note the minute fidelity of the whole picture, and the half-sportive, half-sad tenderness with which he urges "the right divine of helplessness." No man ever lived who loved children more, and was more beloved by them, than Longfellow ; many an eager schoolboy has walked out from Cambridge to get a glimpse of the white-haired poet in his declining years, and though racked by the pain from which he was seldom wholly free of late he never once turned them away disappointed, never once refused to gratify their ardent curiosity.

Born in purple chambers of the morn = born to be the heir to a despotic sovereignty, similar to that exercised by the monarchs of the East (where the morn appears). The word "purple," Lat. *purpureus,* Gk. πορφύρεος, is used by the poets to indicate (1) brightness, (2) royalty—here it indicates both. In " To the Rhine" Longfellow has :—

> "Thou royal river, born of sun and shower,
> In chambers purple with the Alpine glow ! "

And again, in his "Flower de Luce" (*fleur-de-lys*) we have :—

> "Born in the purple, born to joy and pleasance,
> Thou dost not toil nor spin,
> But makest glad and radiant with thy presence
> The meadow and the lin."

A conversation in his eyes—cf. Byron's "Eyes spake love to eyes that spake again." *Conversation* is used by a poetic license for " eloquence." See next note.

The golden silence of the Greek—Homer (Pope's), *Il.* xiv. 252, has

> "Silence that spoke, and eloquence of eyes."

The Germans have a proverb, borrowed from the Greek,—

> "Speech is silvern, Silence is golden ;
> Speech is human, Silence is divine."

Resistless, fathomless, and slow, &c.—Many passages might be quoted from Longfellow's works to show that he was not so deficient in humor as some of his critics allege him to have been. There is a pleasant and homely playfulness about the contrast of the arbitrary power of the young "monarch absolute" with his submission to the "resistless, fathomless, and slow" power over which he can exercise no control. The story of King Canute and his rebuke of the flattery of his courtiers is well known ; Longfellow preserves the verisimilitude of the allusions throughout, even to the minute pushing back of the chair. [' *Rustling* like the sea ' has been objected to by critics who have never heard the sound of the waves as they gently rub together the commingled shingle, sand, and sea-weed at the incoming of the tide.]

IV. This prelude is fairly open to the objection that the effect of the first simile is marred by the introduction of the second ; either would have been sufficient, and either would have been better without the other. Distinguish between *simile* and *metaphor.*

Landscape—originally spelt *landskip*, and meaning the background of a picture ; the word is borrowed from the Dutch painters, from *land* and *shape*. The suffix is the same as *ship* in such words as friend*ship*.

For boughs — on account of, because of—used always with a notion of hindrance or opposition.

The Fairy Isles—the ' Isle of Flowers '—and ' far-off Dreamland ' are of course mere poetic variants for the expression of the same idea. *Fairy*, Low Lat. *fatarium*, from *fatum*, as *prairie*, Low Lat. *pratarium*, from *pratum*.

Pattern girl of girls — A sample, or copy, of what girls should be, really the same word as *patron*—a pronunciation which still holds in provincial English.

Embower'd in curls—The *in* is accounted for by its proximity to the word *embower'd*, though *covered in* curls would neither be bad nor unintelligible English. A. S. *buan* — to dwell, whence *bower*, and *byre* — a stable.

And sailing with soft, silken sails—Name the figure.

Azure eyes of deeper hue—*deeper* than what ? *Azure* properly means *light blue*, from *lazur*, the same word as lapis *lazuli*, Arabic *lájward*, a stone of a light blue color—the dropping of the *l* may be accounted for on the ground of its being mistaken for the article (quasi *l'azur*) and so regarded as insignificant.

Horizon—ὁρίζον, the neuter participle of ὁρίζω = to bound, ὅρος — a boundary. What is meant by ' the horizon of their bowls ? '

The days that are to be—not simply ' the future,' but the days that *will* come regardless of the carelessness of childhood.

V. The mixed simile of the preceding prelude is continued in this, and the continuation is open to the same objection as the introduction ; besides which, this prelude has to bear the burthen of the very far-fetched simile in the last two lines.

Moon's pallid disk is hidden quite — the last word weakens the force of the expression ; *disk*, or *disc*, Gk. δίσκος, Lat. *discus* = a quoit, a round plate ; the word *dish* is merely a softened form.

As round a pebble, &c.—the very essence of the goodness of a simile is that it should closely resemble the thing to be illustrated. In this, the only point of similarity is growth ; or, to give the poet the fullest benefit of all doubt, it is large growth from small beginnings ; but even here the resemblance is far-fetched, unnatural, and unreal ; a table, howsoever 'wider grown,' cannot be compared with the ever widening circles caused by throwing a pebble into water. *Pebble* = a small round stone. Lat. *papula*, through the A. S. *papol*.

Fair Ariadne's Crown.—Ariadne was the daughter of Minos, the celebrated mythical king and lawgiver of Crete. According to the myth, Pasiphaë (= giver of light to all), the wife of Minos, had given birth to the Minotaur by an adulterous intrigue with Taurus, and the monster had been shut up in the labyrinth (of Dædalus), where he was fed on criminals and on the annual tribute of youths and virgins furnished for the purpose by Athens, which had been conquered by Minos. In order to free Athens from the necessity of paying this tax, Theseus, the national hero of the Athenians, visited Crete, was beloved by Ariadne and was by her furnished with a ball of yarn (a clue) by which he was enabled to reach the lair of the Minotaur and to retrace his steps through the winding passages of the labyrinth. On his return he carried off Ariadne with him, but abandoned her on the island of Naxos, where she was found and married by Bacchus on his triumphal return from the conquest of India. Her new god-husband presented her with a golden crown manufactured by Vulcan, which was subsequently transferred as a constellation to the skies, and there it still remains as "Ariadne's Crown."

Flutter awhile, and then quiet be.— Note the truthfulness of the contrast between the conduct of the maidens and the youths, and develop it in a short prose essay.

Van and front of fate—*van*, French *avant*, Lat. *ab ante*. Point out the difference between *van* and *front*. Note that the words are taken in their military sense.

Knight-errantry = tendency to *wander* as the knights of old in quest of adventure. A. S. *cniht* = a boy ; Dutch *knecht* = a soldier, a sense in which the same root is used in the Celtic ; very probably connected with *kin* ; *errantry, error, errare*, has no connection with the word *arrant*, which means, thievish.

E

The lyric Muse == Melpomené (lit. the Songstress, μέλπω == I sing) was the Muse of lyric poetry, more particularly of Tragedy. The *nine* muses of the later mythology were the daughters of Zeus and Mnemosyné (Memory), or Harmony, according to another version ; while still another version makes Harmony the daughter of the Muses, with a disregard to physiological considerations by no means uncommon in mythology. The names of the sacred nine are inserted here for reference :— Clio, Euterpé, Thalia, Melpomené, Terpsichoré, Erato, Polyhymnia, Urania, and Calliopé.

The Phantom—is fame, φάντασμα. Note the liquid softness of the next line, and the energetic vividness of the four following.

VI. This informal simile is more appropriate, and therefore in better taste than those in the preceding preludes ; the image of " the Stream of Time " running " with a swifter current as it nears the gloomy mills of Death," is at once true and expressive, though it is obvious that the " mills of Death " is merely the metaphorical equivalent of the terrestrial mill in the second line. The allusion is to the rapidity with which time seems to fly at the close of life. *Gloomy*, A. S. *glóm* == twilight, cf. ' gloaming.' *Mill* is a corruption of *miln*, Lat. *molina*. *Death* is pure A. S.

Like the Magician's Scroll.—A roll of parchment, contracted from *scroic-el*, a diminutive of *scroic* = a shred, or strip. Magicians were not allowed to use their peculiar powers for their own aggrandizement ; if they did so, the mystic writing — the instrument of their power—disappeared. The comparison in the text is decidedly weak and far-fetched.

Ceylon—Zanzibar—Cathay.— Any other distant places would have suited as well. Where are these places? Cathay, or Kathay, is Marco Polo's name for China, or rather for Chinese Tartary, where he was for many years a resident at the court of Kublai Khan.

Battle's terrible array—obviously an imitation of Byron's

"Battle's magnificently stern array." *Childe Harold*, III. 28.

array, a hybrid formed by prefixing *ar* (= Lat. *ad*) to the Scandinavian *rede* == order. Cf. A. S. *ræde* == *ready*. *Battle*—Old French *bataille* ; Lat. *batalia*.

To lift one hero into fame—infinitive of purpose.

She find — parse. The pathos of this touching picture is worthy of the poet at his best, nor is the language unworthy of the theme.

VII. **The darksome woods**—*dark* and *some* (A. S. *sum*); cf. *fulsome*. "The *darksome* night" occurs in the old ballad, *The Babes in the Wood*.

Drops down—is the equivalent of the Lat. *occidit*, and is descriptive of the *suddenness* with which the sun appears to set (lit. *to fall*) in cloudy weather.

The Golden Wedding-day—is the fiftieth anniversary of the wedding, as the silver-wedding is celebrated on the twenty-fifth anniversary. A. S. *weddian*—to pledge, to engage.

Corridor == a gallery, and hence a long hall or passage like a gallery ; the word is Italian, connected with Lat. *curro* — I run.

Monarch of the Moon—as though the 'Man in the Moon' had visited the earth in the guise of a child "with face as round as is the moon." More than one old nursery rhyme describes such a descent, e.g. "The man in the moon came tumbling down, and asked the road to Norwich," etc.

Ancient bridegroom and the bride.—These words touchingly portray the continuity of their mutual affection ; notwithstanding their long years of wedded life they are to-day as much the bridegroom and the bride as they were on that other "happy day" just fifty years ago. *Bride-groom*, by an improperly inserted *r*, is A.S. *bryd-guma*, i.e. *bride-man*, c.f. *homo*.

Blithe == happy, a pure A. S. term. Cf. also A. S. *blican* == *blincan* == to shine. Eng. *blink*.

Their forms and features multiplied—by being reproduced in those of their children and grandchildren. The simile with which the poem ends can scarcely be regarded as anything but a most "lame and impotent conclusion." The poem might much better have ended with the line just quoted.

ARTHUR HUGH CLOUGH—1819 1861.

"As Ships, Becalmed at Eve." Extract LXIX, page 346.

Biographical Sketch.—In glancing at the careers of the pupils who enjoyed the advantage of Dr. Arnold's tuition and supervision at Rugby, one cannot help being struck by the fact that the example of his manly piety, and the precepts of his admirable homilies, were not enough to guard his charges against the baleful influences of the sceptical age in which their lot was cast ; but at the same time one must acknowledge and acknowledge gladly, that there is nothing underhand, sneaking, unmanly, about the scepticism into which more than one of his favorite pupils unhappily allowed themselves to drift ; and this resolute, almost heroic willingness to face the consequences, to have the courage of their opinions, was no doubt due to the lasting influence of the character of their revered master. ARTHUR HUGH CLOUGH (*Cluff*) was born in Liverpool, England, in 1819 ; accompanied his father, a prosperous cotton merchant, to the United States in 1823, and resided there till 1828 when he was brought back to England and sent to Rugby under the supervision of Dr. Arnold. In 1836 he entered the University of Oxford, where he unaccountably failed to distinguish himself at examinations though he gained a high reputation for scholarship, ability, and probity of character : and in 1842, the influence of Dr. Arnold, with whom he had always been a great favorite, helped him to secure a fellowship, supplemented the next year by a tutorship in the University.   Clough had ever been of an enquiring mind, and the comparative leisure of his position now gave him ample opportunity for at least a superficial examination of some of the dogmas of Christianity.   It was an age of enquiry, a restless, seething, turbulent age of investigation, in which men were no longer content to take the "ipse dixit" of authority as an all-sufficient guide through the mysterious labyrinths of life.   Strauss had published his rationalistic *Leben Jesu*, Carlyle's *Past and Present* was not calculated to give rest on orthodox ground to a soul striving for some unshifting resting-place ; nor had Mill and Spencer in England, nor Comte and George Sand on the Continent, aught but the veriest husks of Positivism to offer to a soul hungering for the bread of life.   There was, it is true, the great Oxford revival of religion—the Tractarian movement—but, unhappily for Clough and the Rugby boys in general, their earlier training and the traditional Broad-churchism of their school, fostered by their idolized Head-master, had predisposed him and them to look with suspicion on a movement that seemed to savor all too much of the spirit of Mediævalism, if indeed it did not aim at a revival of the Romanism into which Newman and some others of the Puseyite revivalists had already drifted. The logic of events has proved the groundlessness of such fears ; but the fears and suspicions were very real and very strong at the time, and so Arthur Clough and others were turned aside from the only school of religious thought in which their æsthetic tastes would have been gratified, while the tangibility (if it may be so expressed) of their religious cult, and the activity, piety, and zeal of the promoters of the new churchism might have saved them from turning for spiritual food to the dry shavings swept out of the back doors of German metaphysical workshops.

In 1848 he resigned his fellowship and other positions and emoluments in Oxford, and shortly afterwards was appointed principal of University Hall, London. In the same year he published his most successful poem, *Bothie of Tober-na-Vuolich*, a poem describing the doings of a Long Vacation reading party, under their ' coach ' *Adam*, on the shores of Lough Ness in Scotland. Longfellow, one of Clough's prime favorites, had published Evangeline during the preceding year, 1847, and it was in the dactylic hexameter of Evangeline that Clough wrote his pastoral idyll. More powerful than the *Bothie*, at least in parts, is the bizarre tragedy of *Dipsychus;* but it is doubtful whether it, or any portion of it, will survive so long as some few of the unpretentious flowers that might be culled from his small garden of poesie, the *Amours de Voyage* and the *Mari Magno.*

In 1852 he visited America, where he met with Longfellow and Emerson, and the following year he returned to London, England, where he had received an appointment in the recently reorganized Education office. To the duties of his office and to the pursuits of literature he devoted himself with as much assiduity as failing health and a constitution never very strong would allow ; and though he stoutly maintained his sceptical views to the end, he did so without bitterness and without intolerance,—holding his own, indeed, with all the energy, but at the same time with all the gentlemanly courtesy, suavity, and grace that might be expected from one of Dr. Arnold's favorite Rugby boys.

What might have been Clough's place in literature had he been spared for the full development of his talents it would be idle to conjecture ; he died of a malarial fever at Florence, in Italy, during a holiday tour in 1861, leaving behind him the reputation of an upright, honest, fearless asserter of his right to differ in opinion from the opinions of others. In this doubting, scoffing age it is well for the cause of orthodox belief that so few of its opponents can exhibit characters to the world as sensitive, as upright, and as pure as that of Arthur Hugh Clough.

AS SHIPS, BECALMED AT EVE.

This extract very fairly illustrates the restless longing after
certainty that formed so marked a characteristic of Clough and
of many of the young Oxford men of his time ; the same rest-
lessness and uncertainty are well exhibited in his "Stream of
Life," and in many other short effusions of his lyric Muse. In
the extract immediately following we can see the bitter scorn with
which he refuses to acquiesce in the mere goody-goody vapid
theories of respectable theology ; and in this, we can discern the
touching sadness with which he finds himself carried so far from
the modes of thought of the companions of his early years. A
fondness for simile, an introspective habit of mind that gives a subjective cast to all his writings, and a careful choice of good, pure,
nervous Saxon English are features of the author's general productions that may be readily enough discerned in these few
stanzas. It will be a useful exercise in composition for the pupils
or students to write a carefully prepared prose paraphrase of the
poem.

With canvas drooping—*canvas* = = hempen cloth ; Lat.
cannabis, Gk. χάννναβις, Persian *kanab*, Sanscrit *cana,* all = - *hemp.*
Parse *side* by side, *towers, scarce, leagues, apart.* League = three
miles, or thereabouts,—connected with Irish *leige*, Lat. *Leuca,*—
not to be confounded with the word *league* = confederacy, Lat.
ligare = to bind, through Italian *lega*, and French *ligue.* *Descried*
--made out, distinguished, French *décrire*, Old Fr. *descrire*, Lat.
describere.

Dawn of day—A. S. *daeg* = day ; *dagian* = to grow bright.
Durkling hours—See note on p. 273 of the H. S. Reader.
Nor dreamt, &c.—A somewhat strong image this, that of a
ship endowed with power to think what the other ship was doing.
But each—by each = nor thought anything, except (but)
that each was cleaving the self-same seas beside the other (by
each).
E'en so—Aposiopesis. The sentiment in this stanza, and
indeed throughout the poem, very closely resembles Coleridge's
exquisite description of the estrangement of friends :—

"Alas ! they had been friends in youth," &c.

Astounded - astonished = astonied. Lat. *extonare*, French
étonner. In meaning the infinitive "to feel" is really the principal verb—absence, when they were joined anew, made them feel
astounded, and estranged. French *étranger*, Lat. *extraneus*, extra.
Or wist—for an older form *wiste*, is the past tense of the verb

to wit, A. S. *witan* == to know : common enough about the period of the authorized translation of the Bible.

To veer, how vain ?—This stanza appears to groan beneath the burthen of an unhealthy fatalism : it would be useless to veer, or alter the course, for the vessels having once drifted asunder can never be brought together in the ocean voyage (of life), though they may together enter the harbor at last.

One compass guides—reason and conscience. What a pity that honest souls like Clough's cannot always accept the compass-regulator—Revelation !

Lead them home—It has been well said that prayer is an instinct of the soul : if we cannot offer the tribute of prayer to the Eternal Author of Nature, instinct compels us to offer it somewhere—to Nature herself for want of some higher Power to be adored.

Methought—See note on p. 89 of H. S. Reader. Notes p. 8.

Where'er they fare—used here in its literal sense—A. S. *faran* == to go.

ARTHUR PENRHYN STANLEY.—1815–1880.

DOCTOR ARNOLD AT RUGBY.—Extract LXXII., page 350.

Biographical Sketch.—Among the valuable legacies bequeathed by Dr. Arnold to the world must be reckoned the broad catholic spirit infused by his example and his precepts into his pupils, so many of whom have become teachers of men, transmitting to the later generations the lessons of manliness, of sympathy, and of tolerant charity that they learned from their great highpriest at Rugby. That they did not all turn out orthodox believers is no argument against their master or his system ; in such an inquiring age it was inevitable that among men of the thoughtful mould of the Rugbæans there should here and there be one who had drifted from the old-time moorings,—and it is indeed matter of wonder, no less than of congratulation, that so many of them were able to " hold fast that which is good " during a period when it was so difficult, so well-nigh impossible, for mere human reason to find a satisfying answer to the despairing cry, " Who will show us any good?" That men like Clough and Matthew Arnold should be sceptical is due to the influences that beset them in their manhood's years, that there was an honest manliness and a courteous tolerance about their scepticism was largely due to the Rugby influences that moulded their characters as boys ; and to the same influence can be traced the muscular Christianity of men like Thomas Hughes, and the broad catholic spirit of such men as ARTHUR PENRHYN STANLEY, the typical representative of the great Broad Church party in the widest, wisest, and best sense of the term.

He was the second son of the Right Reverend Dr. Edward Stanley, Lord Bishop of Norwich, and hence from his infancy was surrounded by an atmosphere of ecclesiasticism that no doubt exercised some influence in determining his future career; he, however, always maintained that the development of his genius, as well as his possession of it, was due much more to the influence of his Welsh mother, with her ardent Celtic temperament, than to the more sober example of his somewhat phlegmatic English father. At the age of fourteen he became a pupil of Dr. Arnold's at Rugby, where he remained for five years, till his matriculation into Baliol College in the University of Oxford. Whether he was the original of the "Arthur" of *Tom Brown's School Days* is of little consequence; he, at all events, like the other Arthur, enjoyed from the first the confidence and esteem, the friendship and the love of his fellow-pupils, his tutors, and especially of the headmaster, whose affection for young Stanley came as near to partiality and favoritism as Arnold's rigid sense of justice would allow. The friendship was fully reciprocated, and in the after years it was fully repaid by the publication of the *Life of Dr. Arnold,* a biography that reflects the greatest credit not only on the author and the subject, but on his old school and school fellows. Stanley's career in Oxford was more than commonly brilliant, his distinctions in classics, English prose and verse composition, and theological subjects being numerous and important. On the completion of his undergraduate course he was elected to a fellowship in University College, where, for some dozen years, he faithfully and zealously discharged the duties of an University tutor, while assiduously prosecuting his researches in ecclesiastical history. In 1858 he was appointed Regius Professor of Ecclesiastical History in his University, and his broad catholicity no doubt acted as a corrective of the exclusive spirit of the High Church party, fostered for the preceding ten years and more by the ability, the integrity, and the energy of Dr. Pusey. On the death of Archbishop Whately, in 1863, the Archbishopric of Dublin, Ireland, was offered to Stanley; but the position demanded peculiar qualities of administrative ability, and a knowledge of Irish character and Irish affairs in which he felt that he was deficient, notwithstanding the Celtic temperament inherited from his mother, and he wisely declined the very tempting offer of preferment. A few months afterwards he was advanced to the dignity of the deanery of Westminster, and here he found himself in his proper position in the world; no other position would have fitted him so well, and no other priest of the Anglican communion would so well have fitted the position at the time.

The somewhat peculiar course of ecclesiastical history in England has resulted in depriving the bishops of all real power in the cathedral churches, of which they were once the real, as they are still the titular, heads; and the force of circumstances has vested this abrogated power in the hands of the dean and chapter; hence it has come to pass that the dean of Westminster Abbey—the great representative church of the Anglican community—exercises a power superior, in many important respects, to that of his bishop, or even to that of the metropolitan Archbishop, and that he is regarded in a peculiar sense as the embodiment and the exponent of the views of the Church of England. Stanley realized the significance of his position from the first; and the unanimous testimony of his contemporaries is that he succeeded beyond all expectation in the attainment of his own high ideal " to make Westminster Abbey the great centre of religious and national life " in the kingdom. To find a resting place amid the hallowed dust of the departed heroes of England, in England's most hallowed shrine, has for ages been the highest ambition of Britain's worthiest sons, and this ambition Stanley was ever careful to foster and encourage; but he did much more than this,—he contrived to impress upon the people that this was their national church, that here the national prayers and praises should be offered, and so he brought it to pass that the services in Westminster Abbey ceased to be a mere perfunctory reading of portions of the Book of Common Prayer, and became in very sooth a veritable power in the land. Regarding the old historic Abbey as the type of the national church, his services and sermons were marked by a broad, all-embracing catholicity, little understood, and still less appreciated, by the narrow-minded bigotry and intolerance of the Extremists. To him, however, it was the temple of the nation, to which all men had a right to go up, and in which all men had a right to worship ; and so he exerted himself, and with singular success, to provide the Bread of Life in such a way as would be most beneficial to his hearers. The rich were warned in special sevices pointing faithfully to their dangers; the poor were, with still greater kindness and sympathy, encouraged to bear up in this world, and to hope for a bright heaven of plenty in the world to come; the artisan was taught that his vocation was no whit less honorable than that of the artist; the peer and the pauper, the countess and the costermonger, the shoe-black of the London streets and the sprightly scions of noble houses, were alike reminded that they would hereafter be compelled to render an account of the deeds done in the body. It was, indeed, an imposing sight to witness, for example, such an occasion as a special sermon by "the Dean" to the newsboys, or to the shoe-blacks, of London—the old Abbey filled with an eager crowd of boys from all the purlieus of the great metropolis, to-day occupying the seats and stalls that had yesterday been filled by the more religious members of the "Upper Ten Thousand " of English aristocracy—and then to mark the deep earnestness of the truly venerable preacher, as he related some story of youthful honor, truthfulness, and heroism, while the tears trickled visibly down his kindly face, and the broken voice of the narrator seemed to be fitly accompanied by the sobbing, the sighing, and the tears of his youthful, sympathizing hearers.

One episode in his career as Dean of Westminster exposed him at the time to a goodly amount of virtuous indignation, viz.: his permitting Bishop Colenso to occupy the pulpit of Westminster Abbey on one occasion, during a temporary visit to England, after the publication and general condemnation of his heretical criticism of the Pentateuch. The circumstances were peculiar : Colenso, Bishop of Natal, had published several volumes attacking the credibility, the genuineness, and the authenticity of the Books of Moses, and thus undermining the authority on which the Church of England is founded ; a storm of very justifiable indignation had gone forth against the heretic; public opinion had condemned him, and nothing but a legal quibble (or what looked very like a legal quibble) had saved him from deprivation of his office and emoluments as a bishop of the Church of England—and yet in the face of all this, in the very teeth of an incensed and outraged public opinion Dean Stanley allowed the proscribed prelate to occupy the pulpit of the representative national church of England. And why? was it from sympathy with Colenso's views, and from a desire to support them? Far from it! Colenso's views were as repugnant to Stanley's as they well could be—in all material points, indeed, they have been proved to be untenable and absurd ; nay, more, had they been true, it does not seem to require any argument to prove that he should not have enunciated them, and at the same time continue to wear the livery and to enjoy the emoluments of the Church whose tenets he had taken a solemn oath to maintain. But, on the other hand, such legal machinery as was available had been put in operation against him, and he had been declared to be by law and usage the rightful Bishop of Natal, and as a prelate of the national church Stanley very properly considered that the pulpit of the national cathedral should be open to him. Moreover, though he had no sympathy whatever with Colenso's views, he was not unwilling to emphasize his belief that freedom of thought was too priceless a boon to be wrested from any man, whether priest or proletariat, at the mere caprice of a fanatical public opinion.

Stanley's published works exhibit the characteristics that marked his life,—an indefatigable love of work, a broad tolerant spirit of charity, a frank and unenvious appreciation of merit. His style is marked by clearness, harmony, and force ; and his numerous works show a depth of learning and research hardly to be expected in such a busy priest of the Anglican Church. In addition to numerous articles in magazines, he wrote *Lectures on the History of the Eastern Church*, of the *Jewish Church*, of the *Three Irish Churches*, and of the *Church of Scotland*. His *Memorials of Westminster Abbey* is a truly valuable contribution to the secular no less than to the ecclesiastical history of the Kingdom, and the *Life of Dr. Arnold*, from which latter publication the extract is taken, is unquestionably one of the best and most discriminating biographies that has ever been written.

In connection with this extract the student should study the brief Biographical Sketch of Dr. Arnold, prefixed to the notes on the extract entitled " Unthoughtfulness," extract XLV., page 227 of the High School Reader.

DOCTOR ARNOLD AT RUGBY.

Dr. Arnold's methods have been so fully discussed in these notes (see p. 31), and the general and special principles of school government have been so clearly enunciated in the Canadian edition of Baldwin's *School Management* that there does not seem to be any reason for entering on a consideration of these subjects here. Besides which, the extract is, like most of Stanley's writings, so clear and self-explanatory that an attempt at elucidation would only serve to remind the reader that :—

> " To gild refined gold, to paint the lily,
> To throw a perfume on the violet,
> To smooth the ice, or add another hue
> Unto the rainbow, or with taper light
> To seek the beauteous eye of heaven to garnish,
> Is wasteful and ridiculous excess."
>
>   SHAKSPEARE, *King John*, IV., 2.

There are, however, two very important questions raised in the extract : (1). Is it right to secure the performance of right actions from wrong motives, under circumstances (as in childhood, for example) in which the right motive would be inoperative ? and (2). Is it possible to shorten the transition period between childhood and manhood without permanent injury and exhaustion of the faculties ? And as these questions must occur in the experience of every teacher, and as opinions must differ very widely as to their answers, it may not be altogether superfluous to comment briefly on them in their proper places in the extract.

Management—is an extension of the older noun *manage* — control of a horse, originally, and then extended to government in general ; cf. Italian *maneggio* = a riding-school, *mano*, Lat. *manus* — the hand, the fundamental idea being that of 'handling.' Not to be confounded with *ménage* = a household. Old French *mesnage*, i.e. *maison-age*.

Not performance but promise.—With this sentiment contrast the sentiments expressed by Longfellow in " The Village Blacksmith," " The Psalm of Life," and elsewhere. Arnold's theory and practice were unquestionably true as regards the true function of school and college ; the object aimed at, even intellectually, should be to teach students how to study for themselves, not to endeavor, as so many teachers are unwillingly forced to do now, to stuff the pupils with encyclopædias of undigested, unassimilated mental food.

Principle—adopted—in training, &c.—i.e. that freedom and independence, though fraught with danger, develop character better than restraint and coercion.

Actions right in themselves — performed from wrong motives—With due diffidence and due deference to the opinions of others the following conjecture is hazarded on this vital point :—*It is right* and proper to enforce actions right in themselves on young children, even though these actions be performed from wrong motives ; and in spite of Dr. Arnold's theory we find that in practice he constantly secured the performance of such actions from motives that could certainly not claim to be the highest,—for example, "there grew up a general feeling that ' it was a *shame* to tell Arnold a lie,' "—and why ? Not from the highest motive, not because lying is forbidden by God, but because it was a violation of Arnold's confidence—"he always believes one." No doubt the appeal should always be made to the highest motives available, but if children cannot be taught the virtue of truthfulness by the consideration that it is a *sin* to tell a lie, they certainly ought to be taught this virtue from the much lower (though, alas ! generally the more efficacious) consideration that the violation of it is a *shame*. The guiding principle in matters of this kind is this :—It is of primary importance to secure the performance of right actions, for performance by constant repetition becomes habit, habit grows into principle, principle is the basis of morals, and sound morals are no insecure foundation for religion. It would be indeed truly delightful if the teacher had only to suggest the possibility of sinfulness as a sufficient deterrent against any course of wrong in his pupils ; but we must be content to take human nature as we find it ; and however utopian our theories, our practice must be mundane.

He writes in 1837—After nine years' experience of the trials and temptations of school-boy life in Rugby.

Corruption of his character—The character is not an inherent quality, it is the distinctive mark, or sign, engraved on the individual as the result of his contact with the world around him. Gk. χαρακτήρ = an engraved mark, χαράσσω = I engrave. The word is often used loosely for ' disposition' as Arnold uses it here.

"Can the change—be hastened—without exhausting the faculties ?" &c.—The importance of finding a correct answer to this question can hardly be exaggerated. Opponents of Arnold's system point to such examples of his teaching as his own son, Matthew Arnold, and Arthur Clough, one of his 'most favored pupils ; but surely it cannot be said that there was any premature exhaustion of the faculties in the case of these men. The fact seems to be that here, as in most disputable questions, the truth lies in the mean between extremes, and every teacher will have to decide in the case of every pupil how far this shortening process can be carried out successfully—how "the assumption of a *false manliness* in boys" can be repressed, and how best "to cultivate in them *true manliness*, as the only step to something higher" and holier in their characters and lives.

Lying to the masters—used to be regarded as a very venial offence by boys, and even by masters, till Arnold's introduction of a new way of looking at such faults. Since his time the old idea of a necessary antagonism between pupils and their teachers has almost entirely disappeared ; and nowadays the true teacher is considered even by the pupils as one who takes as much interest as they do themselves in sustaining and developing the *esprit-de-corps* without which no school can rightly discharge its educational functions. Note how this feeling is attributed by Stanley to his beloved headmaster throughout the extract,—he is "not merely the headmaster, but the *representative* of the school ;" the pupils are "members together with himself of the great institution, whose character and reputation they had to sustain as well as he." In this direction, the creation and fostering of a feeling of pride and affection for the old school, there seems to be room for an almost boundless exercise of enthusiasm and labor ; it is harder to create it in Canada than it was to foster it at Rugby, but with greater permanence in the positions of teachers, and a corresponding increase in their interest in the welfare of their pupils and in the prestige of their schools, it may be hoped that in no long time the annual reunions of old pupils may become as pleasant a feature in the schools of Canada as they are to-day in many of the old public Schools of the dear old Motherland.

GEORGE ELIOT (MARION C. EVANS). 1820-1881.

FROM " THE MILL ON THE FLOSS."—Extract LXXIV, page 356.

Biographical Sketch.— MARION C. EVANS was born in 1820, not far from the manufacturing town of Nuneaton, Warwickshire, England (another account gives Derbyshire as her native county). In 1841, she removed with her widowed father to Coventry, where she resided till his death left her free to gratify her desire for foreign travel and study. From her childhood she was distinguished by an almost passionate love of study, but having no wise counsellor to guide her in the choice of books, her reading was for many years of the most desultory and rarely of the most useful kind. German rationalism took a firm hold on her naturally powerful mind, and at an early age she became distinguished among the *soi-disant* ' advanced thinkers ' of the sceptical school. Though she very seldom obtrudes her " views " on revealed religion, still one can easily read between the lines of her more ambitious productions that they are the work of one who has abandoned the simple faith in which her mother lived and died. It does not necessarily follow that a sceptic in religion should be a scoffer at the decencies of civilized society ; but Marion Evans was too thoroughly radical in her modes of thought not to have had her conduct influenced by her creed ; and so she defiantly flew in the faces of the decent matrons of England, and flaunted it for many years as the avowed paramour of the equally radical essayist, George Henry Lewes. Her first important work was the translation of Strauss's rationalistic *Leben Jesu*, 1846, a work still appealed to as a standard authority by the opponents of orthodox Christianity, notwithstanding the fact that the author has repudiated his early beliefs, and has declared that rationalism is not able to account for the life and labors of Our Lord. This translation and other work of a like kind made her acquainted with the principal literary men of the day, and in 1851 she removed to London as assistant to Dr. Chapman in the editorship of the great radical quarterly, the *Westminster Review*. Three years later, her *Scenes of Clerical Life* appeared in Blackwood's Monthly Magazine, and at once arrested public attention by the clearness and vigor of the style, and by the subtle insight into human character displayed on every page. In imitation of George Sand, the celebrated French authoress, whose *nom de plume* is an abbreviation of the name of her paramour, George Sandeau, Miss Evans also assumed a *nom de plume*, and soon the name of " George Eliot " became as well known in the world of fiction as that of many of its recognized leaders. In *Adam Bede,* in the *Mill on the Floss,* in *Silas Marner, the Weaver,* and in *Felix Holt, the Radical,* she paints the scenes and characters of the rural and manufacturing districts in which her early life was spent ; in *Middlemarch* we make the acquaintance of the Rev. Mr. Casaubon, a divine with more literary ambition than skill, and of his charming young wife Dorothea, with her dreamy and romantic character; *Romola,* an Italian historical novel of the fifteenth century, shows her dramatic power of realizing the manners and customs of a by-gone age ; and in *Daniel Deronda* we have the same minute pre-Raphaelite portrayal of character and manners (Jewish in this case) that distinguishes all her works wherever the scene may be laid.   It has been well pointed out by Mr. Seath in the Advanced Reader of the " Royal Canadian " series, that " subtle and wise reflections introduced as asides to the reader, constitute a marked peculiarity of her style ; " her style is in fact scientific rather than artistic ; she is not satisfied with merely painting a character, she analyzes it, dissects it, performs on it, indeed, a process of moral vivisection that reminds one of a lecture in demonstrative anatomy; and these " asides " are in many cases but the gruesome comments of the lecturer on the moral gangrenes and defective tissues revealed during the process of dissection.   Whether this analytic method will continue to be regarded as artistic, and whether the works of George Eliot will maintain their popularity, after the prevailing rage for Positivism in literature and philosophy shall have died away, are problems that time alone can satisfactorily solve.   One thing at least is certain ; no writer of our age, or indeed of any age, has succeeded so well as George Eliot in imparting a living interest to characters that have so little in common with the ordinary instincts of average humanity; no one has so well painted characters relying entirely for their support on their native human strength, uncheered by the thought of a guardian Providence in this life, unblessed by the hope of a blissful immortality in the life beyond the grave.

SCENE FROM THE MILL ON THE FLOSS.

In this short extract can be seen several of the peculiarities of George Eliot's style ; her tendency to indulge in moralizing ; the marvelous power of word-painting that enables her in a few pregnant words to place a whole scene vividly before the mind ; her subtle insight into the workings of the human mind, and her intense fondness for analytic dissection of her characters.   Mark the truthfulness to nature of the descriptions of the miller's children, the assumption of authority on the part of the boy, and the tendency on the sister's part to submit to a superiority of which she is not less afraid than she is proud. Few writers would have condescended to devote so much attention to a theme apparently so trivial as a fishing excursion by an ignorant pair of children ; but what a charming interlude the incident becomes in the skilful hands of the authoress, and how deftly she intermingles the graces of description, of humor, and of pathos ! The material is not at all promising of good results, but in spite of our knowledge (or suspicion) of this fact, we cannot help feeling a strange wistful pity for poor Maggie, "stepping always by a peculiar gift in the muddiest places," and so serenely happy because on this special occasion her great rough brother "Tom was good to her."

Basket—is a very old Celtic word ; Welsh *basged*, probably connected with Welsh *basg* = a plaiting, which again is possibly connected with A. S. *bœst* ; English *bast*—matting woven from the inner bark of the lime tree. The word is quoted as Celtic by the Latin poets Martial and Juvenal, the latter of whom transfers it as *bascauda*.

Looking darkly radiant.—This *oxymoron* is peculiarly effective in its suggestion of the contrast between her general mood and her present brightness.

Beaver bonnet—The modern silk hat has almost, if not altogether, superseded the beaver hat (the *bever hat* of Chaucer), made, like Maggie's bonnet, of the skin of the beaver, when these sagacious animals were commoner than now. The word *beaver*, however, and even its synonym *castor*, may still be heard as provincial equivalents for "silk hat."

It didn't much matter.—The natural contrast between the tender-heartedness of the girl and the callous indifference of the boy is well expressed. Parse each of these words.

Rather in awe—*rather* is the comparative of an old English word, *rath*, or *rathe*, meaning early, soon. *Rathest* also occurs in old English authors.

Cleverness.—See note on the word 'clever' occurring p. 228 of Reader.

Silly—German *selig*, A.S. *sœlig* = happy, innocent, simple, foolish. Note the degradation in the meaning of the word, as though happy innocence were a sign of folly. Cf. also the note immediately following that referred to in the preceding paragraph.

Punish her when she did wrong.—One of the blurs on the civilization of England is the brutality of the men in the lower ranks of life to their weaker sisters and wives; it would appear quite right and proper to Tom that he should chastise his housekeeper when she did wrong. This brutality is not an indication

F

of cowardice, as it certainly would be elsewhere ; it is simply a lingering remnant of the semi-barbarous feudalism which degraded the women of the lower ranks below the level of brutes: education will slowly remove the stigma, but in the meantime a good, sound, *brutal* flogging would not be a bad corrective of the habit— " *Similia similibus curantur.*"

On their way to the Round Pool—the description is rather from the stand-point of Maggie and the authoress than from that of the more matter-of-fact Tom, to whom its chief recommendation would be, not its mysterious origin or shape, but the fact that the largest fish are to be caught in such deep river pools. For this reason " the old favorite spot always heightened his good humor, and he spoke to Maggie in the most **amiable whispers**," &c.,—in " amiable whispers " for two reasons, first because the fish might hear him if he spoke aloud, and secondly because no true fisherman, like Tom, would expect the fish to come to him if he were cross and out of temper.

Doing something wrong, as usual.—Note the suggestiveness of the phrase, " as usual," conveying as it does the idea of her being accustomed to perpetual fault-finding without any knowledge of the cause.

A large tench bouncing, &c.,—the tench, Lat. *tinca*, through the old French *tenche*, is a fresh water fish of the carp family, to which the well-known gold-fish of the aquarium belongs; he is very tenacious of life, and hence he comes "bouncing on the grass." Observe the fidelity to nature of the boy's pleasure— a lingering trait of the old Nimrod instinct of the human male— and note the contrast between his active eagerness and his sister's passive, dreamy contentment with her surroundings. "Tom called her Magsie," and though she shared but little in his enthusiasm, she "thought it would make a very nice heaven," &c., and so "she liked fishing very much."

No thought that life would change—In this and the two following, concluding paragraphs of the extract, note the utter absence of all thought concerning any but mundane things—an absence (with all deference to George Eliot and her panegyrists) utterly unnatural in children of their age. "Maggie, when she read about Christiana, always saw the Floss"—i.e., the sublime allegory of the Pilgrim's Progress becomes degraded in the child's mind, and instead of the Floss suggesting thoughts of the mysterious river, the reverse process takes place, and when she reads of "the river over which there is no bridge," it becomes transmuted into the tidal stream of her everyday life. So, too, in the lecturer's "aside" of the authoress, moralizing in her own person, the "red-breasts" we used to call "God's birds,"—why? "because they did no harm to the precious crops ! " The language is, indeed, beautiful,—beautiful beyond the reach of cavilling criticism—but its very beauty renders it all the more necessary to be on one's guard lest this subtle essence of Positivism be mistaken for the language of nature and of truth.

Note the vividness of the descriptions and their terseness, and the force and appropriateness of the short similes—" the rushing spring-tide, the awful Eagre,—like a hungry monster," and "the Great Ash, which had once wailed and groaned like a man."

Great chestnut tree—commonly called the chestnut, or chesnut, which should properly be only used of the fruit, or nut, —the tree itself being the *chesten*, Lat. *castanea* (through the French *châtaigne* for *chastaigne*), Gk. Κάστανα, originally the name of a city in Pontus, Asia Minor, where the tree abounded.

Own little river, the Ripple—a tributary of the Floss, taking its name from the *ripples*, or wrinkles, on the surface of a stream flowing over a shallow, gravelly bed. Another form of *rumple*, A.S. *hrympelle* = a wrinkle. Not connected (as Webster, on Trench's authority, gives it) with *ripple* = to scratch slightly, a diminutive of *rip* = to tear.

The Great Floss—properly speaking Floss = a small stream of water—possibly connected with Lat. *fluxus, fluo*—here it is the tidal stream, and it is *great* in comparison with its tributary, " their own *little* river, the Ripple."

The rushing spring-tide, the awful Eagre—the first phrase is the interpretation of the second = the flood-tide moving up an estuary, or a tidal river in an immense wave (sometimes in two or three waves); A.S. *eágor, eár* = water, sea, tidal wave,—the modern *bore*, for which it is used as an equivalent by Dryden. Not connected with the adjective *eager*, Lat. *acer*. *Tide*, A.S. *tíd* = time, hour, season—hence the time between the ebb and flow, and then by an easy transition the ebb and flow itself ; cf. Easter-tide, time and *tide*.

Ash wailed and groaned—the notion is common to the superstitions of most countries. Virgil has the same idea in the Æneid.

Read about Christiana—following in the footsteps of her husband, Christian, as described in the second part of the Pilgrim's Progress, written in jail by the inspired tinker, John Bunyan (1628-1688). Next to the Paradise Lost of Milton, the *Pilgrim's Progress* of Bunyan must be ranked as the great original production of creative genius in the seventeenth century. It was written during the twelve years' imprisonment of its author on a charge of promoting seditious assemblies (1660-1672). Except the

Bible, no work in the English language has been so extensively read as this immortal allegory. What is an Allegory?

Hips and haws on the hedgerows—Note the alliteration —*Hips* are the red fruit of the bramble or wild-rose, or the sweet-briar, A.S. *heóp*; *haws* are the well-known red berry, or rather stone fruit, of the white-thorn, or haw-thorn, so common in the hedges and fences of the Old Country, as the *sloe* is of the black-thorn, A.S. *haga* = an enclosure; *hedgerows*, A.S *hege*, a strengthened form of *haga*, = *haw*. cf. *Ha-ha* == *haw-haw*, a sunk fence.

Red-breasts—take their name of robins from *Robin* == Robert, just as the *daw* becomes the *Jack*-daw; the *pie*, or pye, the *Mag*-pie.

The white star—flowers, &c.,—may either mean the well-known Star of Bethlehem, a white, star-shaped flower, or the more modest starwort, or chickweed; "the blue-eyed Speedwell" belongs to the botanical family of *veronica*. Note that all these things that "are the mother tongue of our imagination" are of the earth, earthy; in the true spirit of Positivism our imagination can only be kindled by experience,—by the past and its associations of ideas; our delight in the ever-changing aspects of nature is due to the remembrance of the delight they gave us in the far-off bygone years,—not at all to the inherent beauty, harmony, and design of nature, still less to the mental association of such attributes with a great Designer, or to the recognition of His power and His love, as manifested in His works. It is unquestionably true that the memory of the joys of childhood vastly enhances the pleasures of contemplation in maturer years; but this is only half the truth, and the exquisite felicity of the language hides the subtle poison of the thoughts, and renders them all the more dangerous for the half-truth they unquestionably embody.

LORD TENNYSON. —1809–

The LORD OF BURLEIGH, AND THE "REVENGE."—Extracts LXXIX, LXXXI., pages 370, 373.

Biographical Sketch.—Alfred Tennyson is the first English poet, the first English writer indeed, who has had conferred on him the doubtful honor of a peerage in recognition of his purely literary merits. Macaulay and Bulwer Lytton had rendered eminent services to their political party, so that their elevation cannot be accepted as a delicate acknowledgement of the claims of literature ; but Tennyson has never been identified with either of the great political parties, nor has he ever taken any active part in the practical politics of the day. Whether the empty title confers honor on him, or he reflects honor on the peerage, is a question of the slightest possible consequence ; but to those who love him best and appreciate him most, "My Lord" will still continue to be known by his old familiar title, plain Alfred Tennyson. He was born in 1809 or 1810, in the parish of Somerby, in Lincolnshire, England ; and here the boy grew up amid the monotonous scenery of the Wolds, the Heaths, and the Fens of his native county, his education being conducted by his father, Rev. G. C. Tennyson, the rector of the parish. In due time he matriculated at Trinity College, Cambridge, where, notwithstanding the disadvantage of having received no previous training at any of the great Public schools, he succeeded in carrying off the Chancellor's prize in English verse awarded on that occasion for the best poem on the somewhat disheartening theme "Timbuctoo." A small volume of poems, written in conjunction with his brother Charles in their boyhood, was his only publication till 1830, when his *Poems, chiefly Lyrical,* appeared, containing " Claribel," " Mariana," and other juvenile efforts at word-painting, with somewhat crude experiments in versification. The volume was received coldly, even harshly, by the critics ; but Tennyson would not allow himself to be discouraged. He continued to write, and his *Poems,* of 1832, show a decided improvement on their predecessors, exhibiting almost in their perfect development the special features that distinguish him from all other poets of his time—the marvelous skill in the selection and management of metre—the exquisite grace and melody of the language—the exuberance of imagery so skilfully interwoven with philosophic reflection and a subtle idyllic power of harmonising the external scenery with the inner thought that has rarely been equalled and has never been surpassed. The sombre monotony of the scenery of Lincolnshire, and the somewhat melancholy introspection common to boys who have been brought up in seclusion, have had their effect on these earlier poems, and the local coloring is not consequently so bright as in his later works, written since his removal to the airy breezes and genial surroundings of the Isle of Wight. The *Lady Clara Vere de Vere*, *The May Queen*, *Œnone*, the *Palace of Art*, and the *Lotus Eaters*, with several other poems in this, his second, volume have been prime favorites ever since their first appearance, and will probably retain their popularity to the end.

His next volume appeared in 1842, containing some characteristic poems, songs, and ballads,—*Locksley Hall*, *The Lord of Burleigh*, the *Mort d'Arthur*—the germ which has since expanded into the noble and majestic *Idylls of the King*—and *The Talking Oak*, perhaps the most markedly Tennysonian of all his works, and one of the few with which the author himself seems to have been perfectly satisfied. *The Princess, a Medley*, 1847, discusses the proper relation of woman to man, and depicts her struggles, hopes, and aspirations with the insight of a philosopher and the tenderness of the true poet.

Tennyson's popularity was now so great that on the death of the aged Wordsworth, in 1850, he was appointed to succeed him in the office of poet laureate—a choice which gave unbounded satisfaction to his numerous admirers. In the same year appeared the most characteristic of his longer works, *In Memoriam*, written to commemorate the untimely death of his bosom friend, Arthur Hallam, the son of the destinguished historian; young Hallam died at Vienna, and the poet endeavours to assuage his grief by giving it vent in this exquisite series of musically uttered reflections on life, death, and immortality. It has been objected to Tennyson—as it had before been objected to Milton on the publication of *Lycidas* to commemorate the drowning of his friend King—that real, heartfelt grief does not express itself in exquisitely polished diction and subtle refinements of reasoning; and that any such labored monument of woe is either a proof of insincerity, or is at best, an indication of a morbid and unhealthy sentimentality. This criticism seems to be at once unjust, ungenerous, and untrue; it appears rather to be true that such elaboration as we have in *In Memoriam* shows that the first keen burst of passionate anguish had yielded to the influence of all-healing time and meditation, and that the poet could now say in very truth :—

> "I hold it true, whate'er befall—
> I feel it when I sorrow most—
> 'Tis better to have loved and lost
> Than never to have loved at all."

Of the series of connected allegories in epic form that make up the *Idylls of the King*, it would be out of place, and probably misleading, to attempt to give any criticism in the limits of a brief note. Each of the *Idylls* takes its fable, or plot, from the legendary lore that has clustered round the name of Arthur, a mythical king of the Britons about the time of the first invasion by the English. These Arthurian legends of the Knights of the Round Table had at one time been chosen by Milton as the subject for a great national epic, but rejected as unfit for his purposes as soon as he discovered their unreal, purely mythical character; this objection has not proved to be an insurmountable barrier to Tennyson, nor to the American poet, Lowell, both of whom have dug some of their choicest gems of poesy out of this seemingly inexhaustibe old mine of fabulous romance.

As a dramatist Tennyson has not succeeded,—that is to say he has failed as yet to produce a good *acting* play; though the exquisite poetry to be met with in passages of *Mary* and of *Harold* would seem to hold out a hope that with greater practical knowledge of stage effect and stage requirements (such practical knowledge as Shakspeare and all other successful dramatists have possessed), he may ultimately succeed in reviving the seemingly lost art of effectively combining true poetry with the scenes and situations demanded for successful dramatic representation.

The position of Poet-laureate is an anomaly and an anachronism in our day, and the sooner it is consigned to the lumber-room of defunct feudalism the better it will be for the poetry and for the common sense of the age. It is a relic of an age even older than feudalism, of a time when every great house maintained its bard to sing the praises of his lord for exploits real or imaginary; and this is presumed to be the function of the laureate to-day—it is his duty to celebrate in song all important events in the history of the royal family, and to compose triumphal odes in commemoration of such heroic deeds as seem to reflect credit and glory on the nation. Such an office was probably a necessity of a barbarous and illiterate age, but it is worse than useless in an age like ours, when for every Agamemnon there are at least a score of Homers. It seems to be the popular opinion that Tennyson has discharged the duties of this anomalous position with singular success—an opinion against which (*pace dixerim!*) a most emphatic protest ought to be recorded. The truth appears to be that Tennyson more than most poets is incapable of manufacturing poetry to order; he cannot summon the Muses at his pleasure, but must wait for the divine afflatus like other gifted sons of Apollo. He can, of course, grind out verses, as could any mere poetaster; but it is surely the very blindness, the self-

abnegation of criticism, hoodwinked by a spurious patriotism, to
dignify by the name of poetry such bombastic fustian as the
Charge of the Light Brigade, or such silly twaddle as the *Welcome
to Alexandra.*

It has been said already that Tennyson takes but little active
part in the practical politics of the day ; but it is by no means to
be inferred from this that he is an indifferent or uninterested
spectator of the events transpiring around him.   On the contrary,
many passages in his poems prove clearly that he takes a keen
interest in the affairs of the nation, and that he interprets the
signs of the times with an accuracy that might well be considered
wonderful in an active partisan politician.   His dedicatory address
to the Queen, for instance, strikes the key-note of the Constitution
as truly as it could be done by a Gladstone or a Beaconsfield :—

> " And statesmen at her councils met
> Who knew the seasons, when to take
> Occasion by the hand, and make
> The bounds of Freedom wider yet
>
> By framing some august decree,
> Broad-based upon the People's will,
> To keep her throne inviolate still,
> And compass'd by the inviolate sea."

THE LORD OF BURLEIGH.

This was one of the poems included in the volume published in
1842, the volume that definitely fixed Tennyson's position as one
of the leading poets of the century, and the not unworthy successor of the gentler section of that band of inspired bards which
included in its ranks Byron, and Shelley, and Scott, and Keats,
and Wordsworth, and Coleridge, and not a few besides.   Most of
these had imbibed the democratic spirit of the age, and their influence may be traced in this and in many others of our author's
minor effusions ; how much this half sympathy with democracy
contributed to his popularity it would be premature now to conjecture, but unquestionably not a little of his success in touching
the hearts of the great middle class of modern English society is
due to the lofty scorn with which arrogant assumption is treated
in not a few of his earlier poems.   The somewhat commonplace
incident of a romantic attachment between a simple village maid
and a lord of high degree has always been a popular one ; and it
must be acknowledged that this almost threadbare theme has been
handled in this poem with singular originality, sweetness, and
success.   The patient, uncomplaining effort of the village maiden
to rise to the dignity of her lordly consort's rank, and her failure

to support "the burden of an honor Unto which she was not born," are wonderfully true to nature, and show that pathos is by no means confined to the atmosphere of the poor ; while the tender anxiety of the husband, and his remorseful acknowledgment that rank cannot bring happiness are set forth in a few delicate touches worthy of Shakspeare himself, and complete a picture of the possibility of wretchedness in high life that goes a long way to reconcile the proletariat to regard complacently the gilded externals of the peer. Scant justice has been done by the critics to this tendency in Tennyson to preach the doctrine that real happiness and worth lie not in the externals, but in obedience to the dictum that "'tis only noble to be good."

The metre of this extract is Trochaic, with alternate rhymes, — the odd lines being Trochaic Tetrameter, and the even being the same metre lacking one syllable, i.e., Trochaic Tetrameter Catalectic (four Trochees wanting one syllable), or Trochaic Trimeter Hypermeter (three Trochees with one syllable over). It is a mistake to suppose "that the alternate lines are *often* a syllable short," that is, that they are intended to be Tetrameters, but "are often a syllable short." There is no such variation in the metre of the poem ; it is as stated above—odd lines, Tetrameter ; even lines, Tetrameter Catalectic throughout the poem. The classical student will notice the difference between the classical and English use of the compounds of the word *metre*,—in English four Trochees in the line or verse are called Trochaic Tetrameter (= four metre), each foot, Trochee in this instance, being considered a metre ; but in classical poetry four Trochees would be called Trochaic Dimeter (= two metre), two feet in dissyllabic verse being regarded as one metre.

In her ear he whispers gaily.—Note the abruptness with which the story commences, the rapidity with which the incidents follow each other, and the concise directness of the 'Speeches' as well as of the narration, all of which is strictly in the spirit of the old ballad style.

In accents fainter.—*Accents* = tone of voice, a common usage in poetry ; *fainter*, as is becoming in a modest maiden responding to the more outspoken declaration of her manly lover.

Love like thee.—*Like* is here an adverb, followed by a dative object, after the analogy of the usual construction with the adjective *like;* it is not 'improperly' used as a proposition, or an adverbial conjunction, as some explain it.

A landscape painter.—The disguise of a travelling artist is common in fiction. *Landscape* is a term borrowed from the Dutch painters ; *land*, and the suffix *schap* = A. S. *scipe* — English *ship*, as in friend-*ship*, town-*ship* ; cf. *shape*.

Lips that fondly flatter.—Note the alliteration in this line and the next.

Leave her father's roof.—The common practice in her rank of life ; but mark the touching confidence in her lover's truth involved in her readiness to "leave her father's roof," in ignorance of the whereabouts of "that cottage Where they twain will spend their days."

Wife—A. S. *wif* a woman, a married woman ; usually, but erroneously derived from A. S. *wefan* — to weave, from which comes *webba*, masc. — a weaver; fem. *webbestre*, which is certainly not a doublet of *wife;* the word is from the Aryan root *wip* = to tremble, to be timid.

By parks and lodges going.—By = past ; *lodges* are the cottages built beside the park gates as dwellings for the gate-keepers.

Made a murmur in the land.—Again observe the ono-matopoëtic effect of the liquid alliteration ; *in the land* is a common enough poetic synonym for 'through the country.'

Says to her that loves him well.—Deception is always dangerous, and hence the lord of Burleigh has cause for his "deep thought," now that he finds himself approaching the revelation ; hence, also, there is a poetic necessity that the reader, no less than the hero, should be reminded that she "loves him well"—so well that she is enabled, for a time at least, to bear up against the shock of discovering that her sweet dream of love in a cottage, for which she was eminently fitted, had to be abandoned for the colder splendors of life in a mansion, for which she was utterly unfit ; the phrase, instead of being a mere excrescence, is one of those subtle touches that reveal the instinct of the true poet.

Lovingly converse—with her.

Betwixt—the *betwixe* of Chaucer ; A. S. *betweox, be* = by, and *tweohs*, a strengthened form of *twá* = two, the feminine, the masculine being *twain*. A.S. *twegen.*

Order'd gardens = Arranged in an orderly manner ; cf. "She will *order* all things duly."

Evermore - continually ; A. S. *œfre.* What would be the meaning of *ever more ?*

Gaze = to look steadfastly, shows the firmness of her belief ; Swedish *gasa* = to stare.

O but she will love him truly.—The syntax of the word *but* may seem a little obscure, appearing, as it does, to be almost an interjection rather than a conjunction; Latham's dictum that conjunctions only connect propositions, or sentences, does not appear to be warranted by the facts of our own or other languages—e.g. in the sentence "two and three are five," it is not true that this is a merely compendious statement of the propositions "two makes five" and "three makes five," which are manifestly untrue, nor will it do to say that it is a short way of saying "two is a part of five," &c., for this is not what is intended—again, in the sentence "the husband and wife are a happy pair," it will not do to say that either, separately, is "a pair," much less "a happy pair," for the idea of "pair," and still more "happy pair," can only be predicated of the subjects in their conjoined relation, so that in these and many similar instances it is the *subjects*, and not the propositions, that are united by the conjunction. Conjunctions, therefore, unite not only sentences, but clauses, phrases, and words, or parts of speech, of any kind—still further, they may *connect an expressed statement with an unexpressed mental conception*; the mind may be dwelling on a train of thought, and during the cogitation the thinker begins to give utterance to his thoughts in words, connecting the spoken or written words by a *conjunction* with the unspoken thought that has given rise to the language. This is a very common thing in our old ballads, many of which begin with an introductory "and," or some other *meditative connective*, e.g.,—

"And must Trelawney die," &c.,
"And art thou gone, my milk-white steed?" &c.

So in our text, the *but* connects her ideas as they are expressed in the poet's words with the unspoken thoughts suggested by the scenes of cheerless, loveless grandeur through which she had been passing—" these halls are very grand, and her young husband might possibly feel some desire to enjoy such splendors, and so might not altogether relish the prospect of love in a cottage, **but** she will love him truly," &c. Many apparent obscurities of Syntax may be very easily explained by keeping in view this mental connection between an unexpressed idea and the expression in words to which the thought has given rise.

He shall have a cheerful home ;—note the uses of *sha l* and *will* in this passage, and also the employment of the "historic present," *cheerful*, from old French *chiére* == the face, countenance, Low Lat. *cara* = the head, face, cf. Lat. *cerebrum*, Gk. κάρα, Sanscrit *çiras*.

Armorial bearings—the separate emblems which together make up the coat of arms, or escutcheon (Lat. *scutum* == a shield), very commonly carved on the keystone of the arched gateway leading to what Eliza Cook describes as the " Stately Homes of England."

Mansion more majestic—what figure of rhetoric? Lat. *mansio, manere*.

Many a gallant, gay domestic—two explanations have been offered of this construction; the first makes *many* a noun, French *mesnie* household, number of servants, followed by the preposition *of* governing a succeeding *plural* noun; but the *of* being corrupted into *a*, and the *a* being mistaken for the so-called article, caused the plural to be changed into the singular form; the other explanation makes *many* A.S. *manig*, and an adjective connected with a root *mag* much or many, common to all the Aryan languages —thus *many* and *a* are both adjectives qualifying the following nouns—**gallant** old French *galant*, *galer*, to rejoice, refers to the dress, cf. *galaday*; **gay**, old French, *gai*, A.S, *gan* = to go, refers to the disposition, cf. the slang phrase, " full of *go;*" **domestic** a *house* servant, used here in its literal sense.

Speak in gentle murmur.—Note the peculiar beauty and effectiveness of the onomatopœia secured by the liquids, exhibiting that ultra-respectful acquiescence of the well-trained English domestic in every suggestion of his master; he does not speak out, he merely " gently murmurs" his assent. Point out any defects in the rhyme, here or elsewhere, in the poem.

"All of this is mine and thine."—Supply the ellipsis. Why not "thine and mine?"

In state and bounty—maintaining the external parade suitable to his rank, but relieving it by the bounty (Fr. *bonté*, Lat. *bonitas*, goodness), of charitably dispensing aid to the poor.

Fair and free—the alliteration is neat, but the phrase, copied from old ballad minstrelsy, adds little or nothing to the effect of the description. To tell us that Burleigh is fair to look upon and is, moreover, unencumbered, or to say that its lord is handsome and open-handed, after the minute preceding details, would be suspiciously like *bathos* in a poet inferior to Lord Tennyson.

Her spirit changed.—Note the variations of tense, and the rapidity of movement in these lines, admirably suggesting such an agitated condition of the mind as he is desirous of describing.

Did prove—not a very elegant equivalent for *became*, Lat. *probare.*

A gentle consort made he—this quasi-intransitive use of make is becoming obsolete.

The people loved her much—one of the Tennysonian tests of true nobility; compare his

> "Kind hearts are more than coronets,
> And simple faith than Norman blood."
>
> LADY CLARA VERE DE VERE.

Perplex'd—bewildered. Lat. *perplexus, per* and *plecto* = entangled.

Burden—This word is usually given in grave poetry under its other form, *burthen*, when used as here in a metaphysical sense.

As she murmur'd = said in gentle tones, not complainingly, as is its usual meaning—cf. "And they speak in gentle murmur."

Which did win my heart—the use of *which* relating to persons is Archaic, and so suits the old ballad style of the poem; it was formerly common in this use, cf. the opening sentence of the Lord's Prayer. A.S. *hwile*, contracted from *hwilic*, *hwi* = why, and *lic* = like.

Droop'd and droop'd—Mark the effect of the repetition here, and in "*faint and fainter*" above, as in " *weeping, weeping* late and early." What is this figure of speech?

Lord of Burleigh –What historical personage had this title? Where is Stamford, or "Stamford-town?"

"**Bring the dress,**" &c.,—the remorseful memory of the past is expressed in these two lines with more pathos than could have been exhibited by the most labored description. Indeed, the depth of tenderness in these last eight lines is worthy of Tennyson at his best, and is an excellent copy of the cadence and the spirit of our best old ballads.

THE "REVENGE." A BALLAD OF THE FLEET. 1591.

Extract LXXXI., page 373.

This spirited war ballad, written in imitation of the old ballads so popular at one time in the army, and still so popular in the navy of Great Britain, is an almost literal account in verse of an historical incident that occurred during the protracted struggle, in the reign of Queen Elizabeth, between the English and their natural enemies, the Spaniards.

Elizabeth had fitted out a royal squadron of seven ships (under the command of Admiral Lord Thomas Howard, with Vice-Admiral Sir Richard Grenville as second in command), to intercept the Spanish West Indian fleet of treasure ships and merchantmen ; but Philip, apprised of their mission, sent a fleet of fifty-five sail of the line to convoy his treasures to Spain. The admiral, not daring to risk an engagement against such fearful odds, returned with six vessels in safety to England,—having failed indeed to *capture* the treasure, but having succeeded in delaying the starting of the Spanish fleet so long that they were compelled to encounter the stormy season of the Atlantic and the Bay of Biscay, so that most of the treasure sank to the bottom of the sea in the shipwrecked vessels that carried it. •

The best account of the special exploit commemorated in the ballad —probably the most memorable sea-fight on record, and in many respects far transcending the most brilliant achievement of even the invincible Nelson—is given by the Rev. Richard Hackluyt (1553-1616), in his *Voyages*, narrating the exploits and explorations of the English. Hackluyt's account is followed by all our later historians, the best abridgment of his narrative being given by Hume, as follows :—

"He [Sir Richard Grenville] was engaged alone with the whole Spanish fleet of fifty-three sail, which had ten thousand men on board ; and from the time the fight began, which was about three in the afternoon, to the break of day next morning, he repulsed the enemy fifteen times, though they continually shifted their vessels, and boarded with fresh men. In the beginning of the action he himself received a wound ; but he continued doing his duty above deck till eleven at night, when, receiving a fresh wound, he was carried down to be dressed. During this operation he received a shot in the head, and the surgeon was killed by his side. The English began now to want powder ; all their small arms were broken or become useless ; of this number, which were but a hundred and three at first, forty were killed, and almost all the rest wounded ; their masts were beat overboard, their tackle cut in pieces, and nothing but a hulk left, unable to move one way or other. In this situation Sir Richard proposed to the ship's company to trust to the mercy of God, not to that of the Spaniards, and to destroy the ship with themselves, rather than yield to the enemy. The master gunner, and many of the seamen, agreed to this desperate resolution ; but others opposed it, and obliged Grenville to surrender himself prisoner. He died a few days after ; and his last words were : 'Here die I, Richard Grenville, with a joyful and quiet mind ; for that I have ended my life as a true soldier ought to do, fighting for his country, queen, religion, and honor : my soul willingly departing from this body, leaving behind the lasting fame of having behaved as every valiant soldier is in duty bound to do.' The Spaniards lost in this sharp, though unequal action, four ships and about a thousand men. And Grenville's vessel [the "Revenge"] perished soon after with two hundred Spaniards in her."

It will be seen that Tennyson follows the foregoing narrative pretty closely ; and it will be a good exercise for the pupils to compare the poem with the prose account, giving parallel quotations, and pointing out any minor discrepancies that may be observed. Note that poetry is not expected to be as accurate as prose in its employment of ⋆Arithmetic, etc. ; it speaks in round numbers rather than in minute detail. Point out instances in the extract.

The metre is very irregular, but by no means unpleasant to the ear. It consists mainly of Trochaics, interspersed with Anapæsts and Iambics, having occasionally a redundant *initial* syllable (*anacrūsis*), and frequently an excessive *final* syllable (*hypermeter*, or *hypercatalectic*). The lines, too, are in many cases made up of two parts, both hypercatalectic ; e.g. ll. 3, 5, 6, 7 :—

> " Spánish | shíps of | wár at ‖ séa ! ‖ wé have | síghted fífty ‖ thrée ‖."
> " Bút I | cánnot | méet them ‖ hére, ‖ fór my | shíps are | oút of ‖ géar ‖."
> " Aúd the | hálf my | mén are ‖ síck. ‖ I must | flý, but | fóllow ‖ quíck ;
>   Wé are | síx ships | óf the ‖ líne ; ‖ cán we | fíght with | fífty ‖ thrée ? ‖ "

In these and many other lines of the poem the emphasis on the redundant syllables obviously prevents us from considering the metre as iambic ; and the same consideration determines the metre of each of these half lines to be trochaic *trimeter* hypercatalectic (= three trochees with accented syllable over) rather than trochaic *tetrameter* catalectic (= four trochees lacking a syllable). The combination of trochaic with iambic metre is very ancient and very wide spread,—especially in the form of three iambic feet, with syllable over, followed by three trochees. This is the old *Saturnian* metre of the Romans ; compare, e.g., the well-known retort of the family bard of the Metelli to the lampoons of Nævius :—

> " Dabúnt | malúm | Metél | lí ‖ Naévi | ó po | étæ ‖."

Compare, also, our own old nursery song :—

> " The queén | was ín | the pár | loúr, ‖ eáting | breád and | hóney ‖."

The same Saturnian metre gives effect to the celebrated Spanish poem of the *Cid*, and to the equally famous German epic, the *Nibelungen Lied ;* and its old familiar cadence may be detected in very many of our older ballads, imitated here so successfully by Tennyson.

The " Revenge "—A ballad of the Fleet, 1591. Revenge, French *re*, and *venger*, Lat. *vindicare*. What is the distinction between *revenge* and *vengeance* ? **A ballad** —This title is the proper one for such a short lyrical epic as we have here. The two primary subdivisions of lyrical poetry were the *ballad* and the *song*, the former intended for *recitation* with or without the accompaniment of the *lyre* or other musical instrument, while the latter was intended to be *sung*, as the name implies—French *ballade* = a dancing song, from the Provençal *ballada*, Low Lat. *ballare* = to dance, cf. *ball* = a dancing party. Milton, following the Italian form, *ballata*, with his usual fondness for that language, has *ballats*, and *ballatry*, still surviving in *ballet*, a special kind of choral dance.

The Fleet, i.e., the royal navy, at the time of the Armada, three years before 1591, "consisted only of twenty-eight sail, many of which were of small size ; none of them exceeded the bulk of our largest frigates, and most of them deserved rather the name of *pinnaces* than of ships."—*Hume.*

At Flores in the Azores.—Shortly after the events here described, Sir Martin Frobisher captured a richly-freighted Spanish vessel, and sunk another, in one of those privateering expeditions that became so popular and so profitable during the years immediately subsequent to the defeat of the " Invincible Armada." The name *Azores* is said to be derived from *açor* -a hawk, in consequence of the numbers of these birds found there on the discovery of the islands. Find the exact position of these and the other places named in the extract.

A Pinnace == used here to signify a small ship (cf. note from *Hume,* above) now used as the name of the second largest of the boats of a man-of-war —originally made of *pine,* whence the name —Lat. *pinus.* Name the other boats of a war-ship.

Lord Thomas Howard.—Name other men of this name, distinguished in war, in literature, and in social science, respectively. Who was Lord Howard of Effingham ?

Coward—derived by the addition of the suffix *ard* to the old French *coc* · = Italian *coda* == Lat. *cauda,* a tail—the meaning being (1) an animal that hangs its tail ; or (2), according to Wedgwood, "like a hare," this timid animal being called *coward,* i.e., " bob-tail," in the old language of hunting ; or (3), it may simply mean " one who turns tail."

Out of gear—Not sufficiently prepared with tackle and other requisites —the original notion is 'preparation' .cf. *yare* == ready —A.S. *gearwe* ·· = preparation, dress, ornament.

Quick—Parse this word. What was its original meaning ? cf. "the *quick* and the dead," '*quick*-silver,' '*quick*-set hedge.' A.S. *cwic.*

Six ships of the line—this does not exactly agree with Hackluyt's account ; *see* introductory note, above. The largest vessels are called 'liners,' ' line of battle ships,' or, as here, 'ships of the line' because in a sea-fight they form in line of battle, while the lighter and swifter frigates undertake the special duty of watching and reporting the movements of the enemy, besides aiding their consorts in the battle. *Frigate* comes to us from the old French *frégate,* Italian *fregata,*—words of doubtful origin, but possibly connected with *fargata,* Lat. *fabricata, fabricare* == to build. Florio defines frigate - " a spiall ship," obviously with the same idea of their functions as that held by Lord Nelson, who used to call them " the eyes of the fleet."

NOTES ON "THE REVENGE." 97

"You fly them for a moment to fight with them again."—It was certainly no sign of cowardice to retreat before such fearful odds ; cowardice did not run in the blood of the Howards, and it was his duty to save his little squadron, forming one-fourth of the royal navy, 'to fight again.' With the sentiment of this line compare the oft-quoted :—

> "He who fights and runs away
> May live to fight another day."
>
> GOLDSMITH, *Art of Poetry.*

Goldsmith no doubt plagiarised from RAY's *History of the Rebellion* (1752):

> "He that fights and runs away
> May turn and fight another day ;
> But he that is in battle slain
> Will never rise to fight again."

Ray plagiarises from BUTLER's incomparable satire *Hudibras:*—

> "For those that fly may fight again,
> Which he can never do that's slain."

And Butler, in turn, got the idea from UDALL's translation of ERASMUS's *Apothegms,*

> "That same man, that runnith awaie,
> Maie again fight another daie."

Tennyson may well be excused for trying a new version of such a string of plagiarisms.

"These Inquisition dogs and the devildoms of Spain."—When Elizabeth was artfully kindling the spirit of her people to resist the Armada, among other devices she took care that "the horrid cruelties and iniquities of the Inquisition were set before men's eyes : A list and description was published, and pictures dispersed, of the several instruments of torture with which, it was pretended, the Spanish Armada was loaded."—*Hume.* It is no wonder, therefore, that the sturdy patriots who then manned the fleet of England, should have been inspired with a hatred of Spain, that rendered them not unwilling to take such chances as have immortalized Sir Richard Grenville and his sublime crew on the "Revenge." Courts of *Inquisition* were established in several states of Europe, for the purpose of *inquiring into* and dealing with offences against the established religion, long before the founding of the general Inquisition in Spain—the first being the one established in the 13th century in France immediately after the subjugation of the heroic Albigenses. The supreme general court of Inquisition was established, in 1484, in Seville, by the celebrated Queen Isabella, aided by Cardinal Pedro Gonzalez de Mendoza,—its first president, or inquisitor-general, being the noto-

G

rious Thomas de Torquemada, the prior of a Dominican convent, who succeeded in securing to his own order a preponderating influence in the management of this *Holy Office ;* it was abolished by Napoleon I. in 1808 ; restored by Ferdinand III. in 1814 ; abolished again by the Cortes in 1820, and since then it has only lived in the memory of those who cannot help occasionally dwelling in thought on the awful horrors of its career, now happily ended forever. There is still, however, at Rome, an Inquisition, or congregation of Cardinals *of the Holy Office*, founded in 1542, to which all the minor Inquisitions of the Catholic world have been made subject ; it takes cognizance of ecclesiastical delinquents, but seems to have neither the power nor the inclination to deal severely with the errors of lay offenders. **Devildoms** may either mean *devilries*, i.e. devilish practices, or, by a much more forcible interpretation, rule of devils. Cf. " Don or devil," below.

Past away with five ships—*Past* is archaic for *passed*, and is allowable in an imitation of the old ballad ; **five ships** shows that the ' six ships' of the first stanza do not include the " Revenge," but that Tennyson has diverged from the generally accepted account.

Ballast—is like many other nautical terms borrowed from the Dutch ; the word is common also in Scandinavian = *bay last*, or back load—*bay* back, or rear, and *last* - - load, or burden, i.e. " a load in the back, or rear (stern), of the vessel," so placed to raise her bows. **Below** = on the lower deck, or hold.

To the thumbscrew and the stake, for the glory of the Lord—Common implements of torture in the practice of the *officials*, or *familiars*, of the Inquisition. Supply the ellipsis before *for*.

A hundred seamen—See introductory note.

Huge sea-castles—Many of the Spanish vessels were four-deckers, a circumstance which placed them really at a disadvantage in a cannonading conflict, for their high-mounted guns fired over the much smaller ships of the English—as had been proved during the running fight between the Armada and the pigmy vessels opposed to them in the channel.

" **We be all** "—an archaic form still found in provincial usage. Note the abruptness of question and answer.

Bang—cf. the old Irish *bong* = to hammer, to beat violently ; the same word occurs with the same meaning in the Scandinavian dialects, and even in the Sanscrit—it is probably of imitative, or onomatopoetic, origin.

Dogs of Seville—the old capital of Spain, and site of the Inquisition,

Don or devil—Note the alliteration. **Don** = Lat. *dominus*, originally a Spanish title of nobility, but used for centuries by

the English-speaking races as a synonym for 'Spaniard.' **Devil**—
a word common to the languages of Europe = calumniator, slan-
derer, Gk. διάβολος: it is not an uncommon thing for those of
one religion to regard all who oppose their beliefs as 'children of
the devil.' In *children*, we have a double plural in the endings,
child-er-en, if not a triple one in the changed vowel sound also.—
See Latham.

Spoke—laugh'd—roared a hurrah—A slightly obscure
climax, but not the less effective on that account. " *We* roar'd "—
observe that the ballad is supposed to be recited by a survivor of
that most glorious of sea-fights.

Ran on sheer into the heart, &c.—Generally the term
sheer is applied to a vessel deviating or turning aside from her
course,—Dutch *scheren* == to go awry ; but if Tennyson is carrying the picture as clearly as he usually does in his mind's eye, he
uses the word in a sense more common in other things than in
relation to nautical matters, i.e. straight ahead, *not* deviating—
" the Spaniard came in sight upon the weather-bow " so that the
" Revenge " might choose " shall we fight or shall we fly ? " The
question was decided in favor of fighting, " and so the little ' Revenge' *ran on* sheer (straight) "—with " half of their fleet to the
right and half to the left."

Mountain-like—is in harmony with the style of the old
ballads ; **up-shadowing**—strikes the ear as a Tennysonian and
modern compound.

Took the breath from our sails, and we stay'd—
Note how graphic this expression is made by the employment of
" breath " for " wind," as though the little vessel were instinct
with life, *breathing* through her sails ; note also the pithy terseness of the conclusion, " and we stay'd."

Like a cloud—Compare this phrase with the same phrase
in the third stanza—the one disappearing gently, this other about
to burst in thunder on their heads.

Four galleons drew away—probably the four lost during
the fight (see introductory note) ; they would naturally *draw
away* in the vain hope of repairing damages. *Galleon*, Spanish
galeon = a large galley, Low Lat. *galea*. Of unknown origin ; but
may it not be connected with the Spanish, Portuguese, and Italian
gala, old Fr. *gale* = ornament, as in *gallant*, *gala*-day, etc.—the
meaning being an ornamented, well-equipped ship. Shakspeare
has " good and *gallant* ship," and the epithet is very common
in our sea-songs.

Larboard—starboard—the left and right sides of a ship,
respectively, as one looks from the stern to the bows. *Larboard*
(now called the *port* side) is *laddebord* in middle English, which

is possibly from Swedish *ladda*, A. S. *hladan* — to lade, load, and *bord* side. Skeat conjectures that the term may have been derived from the custom of stowing the sails, when taken down, on that side, so as not to interfere with the helmsman who stood on the right, or *starboard* side, but does not the equivalent term *port* suggest that it was an early usage to carry the bulk of the cargo on that side, for the same reason? so that the *port* or *larboard* (*laddebord*) is the *load* (or cargo) *side*. Starboard, A. S. *steór* = a rudder, and *bord* = side of a ship: the steersman used to stand on the right side of the vessel, guiding her with a paddle before the introduction of the helm.

Having that within her womb, &c. = having been so riddled— probably set on fire—and so many of her crew being killed by our deadly broadsides. **Aboard** on board.

For a dozen times.—See introductory note.

Musqueteers.—A form copied from Butler's *Hudibras* for the more common *musketeer*; *musket*, old French *mouschet* is transferred to the fire-arm from its original meaning of 'sparrow-hawk,' or 'fly-hawk.' Lat. *musca* = a fly, cf. *mosquito*—just as *falconet*, the name of another early fire-arm is from *falcon*.

As a dog that shakes his ears—the contempt implied in this simile is the only real point of resemblance.

And the sun went down.—Note the beauty of the alliteration and of the rhythm in this line, and the first line of the next stanza?

Ship after ship, &c. —What rhetorical figure in ll. 3, 4, 5 of this stanza.

Dead and her shame.—What shame?

A grisly wound.—A.S. *gryslic* = horrible. *See* introduction.

All in a ring.—Parse *all*. **Seeing forty—were slain.**—Parse *seeing*.

Fought such a fight—*cognate* object. **Sink me**—*dative* object.

The stately Spanish men.—The chivalrous courtesy of the Spanish is well expressed in this and the following stanzas. Rewrite them in prose.

For aught they knew.—*Aught* = a whit, A.S. *a* = one, and *wiht* = creature, person, thing: *ought* is another form of spelling = *o whit*, i.e., one whit.

Sail'd with her loss.—Not only after her defeat and the loss of her English crew, but to the destruction and loss of herself and the two hundred ill-fated Spaniards on board.

Or ever—for *or e'er*, an expression arising by mistake from the common early form *or ere*, in which the *ere* is a mere reduplication and explanation of the *or*, A.S. *ær* = ere. Shakspeare has *or ere* frequently, though *or ever* also occurs in Hamlet:—" Or ever I had seen that day!"

Note the poetic justice of the destruction that " fell on the shot-shattered navy of Spain;" "the lands they had ruined" generate the gale by which the waves are raised to complete the destruction begun by the shot and shell of the "Revenge."

JOHN RUSKIN.—1819-

Of the Mystery of Life, *From* Sesame and Lilies.   Extract
LXXXVII, page 390.

Biographical Sketch.—The nineteenth century has been
prolific in great teachers and preachers of codes of ethics, rules of
life, standards of excellence in art, science, morals, and what not ;
but few of these prophets of the new dispensation have delivered
their messages in such forcible, harmonious, and instructive language as has the author of *Sesame and Lilies.* So seductive,
indeed, is the charm of the language, that the reader is not seldom
induced to allow his imagination to triumph over his judgment,
and to adopt his author's views in obedience to the allurement of
the words rather than from any settled conviction of their truth.

John Ruskin was born in London, England, in the year 1819,
his father being a wealthy merchant, by whose liberality he was
enabled to follow, from his earliest years, the artistic bent of his
genius and inclination.   Entering Christ Church, Oxford, at the
usual age, he carried off the Newdegate prize for English verse
in the year 1839, and graduated in 1842.   Thenceforth he devoted himself with ardor to the study and practice of painting,
his proficiency in which, combined with an unsurpassed command of the English language, soon placed him at the head of
the modern school of art criticism.   In 1867 he was appointed
Bede lecturer in the University of Cambridge ; and a few years
later Slade professor of art in his own *alma mater*, Oxford,—in
both which positions he exercised a powerful influence in guiding
and moulding the modern movement in favor of "æsthetic culture,"
constituting himself, in his lectures as well as in his books, the
champion of pre-Raphaelitism and Gothic architecture.

During his undergraduate career, some adverse criticism of
Turner's landscape painting provoked him to reply in a series of
letters, which ultimately expanded into *Modern Painters*, the first
and greatest original estimate by an English art critic of the relative merits of the ancient and modern schools of landscape painting.   The first volume, published in 1843, stoutly asserted the
superiority of Turner and the modern school ; but the discussion
carried him far beyond the original theme of the letters, and
expanded into five volumes (1843-1860), in which he was led on
to a philosophical consideration of the general principles of art,
and to a highly imaginative description of the mysteries of nature
and their symbolical reproduction in art.

In *The Seven Lamps of Architecture*, in the *Stones of Venice*,
both of which he illustrated with beautiful, original drawings, and

in his *Lectures on Architecture and Painting* he advocates the
Gothic style in architecture, as he advocates pre-Raphaelite principles in art in the "Modern Painters," in *Pre-Raphaelitism*, and
in other works ; while in these, as indeed in all his works,—*The
Ethics of Dust, The Crown of Wild Olive*, and the rest of them,
—he preaches of the mystical union between Nature and Art, and
pleads eloquently for the combination of Beauty and Utility.
Notwithstanding the unfailing charm of his style, it must be
acknowledged that the great critic's later works exhibit a certain
querulousness and intolerance not to be found in his earlier productions ; and as he resembles Carlyle in his hatred of sham, so
also does he resemble the great "sage of Chelsea" in the virulence
with which he denounces it.

To the young student who may be inclined to believe that the
graces of composition are of spontaneous growth, it may not be
unprofitable to quote what Ruskin himself tells us in his *Fors
Clavigera*, of his mode of literary workmanship :—" My own work,"
he says, " was always done as quietly and methodically as a piece
of tapestry. I knew exactly what I had got to say, put the words
firmly in their places like so many stitches, hemmed the edges
of chapters round with what seemed to me graceful flourishes,
touched them finely with my cunningest points of color, and read
the work to papa and mamma at breakfast next morning, as a girl
shows her sampler."

OF THE MYSTERY OF LIFE.

It would not be easy to make a selection of many extracts of
equal length exhibiting Ruskin's style more faithfully than it is
exhibited here. His wonderful mastery of the language enables
him to choose the words that most fitly express the thought, and
his poetic imagination pictures forth his theme with a richness of
suggestive imagery that makes one almost believe that one can see
behind the veil. The extract, however, also illustrates what seems
to be the characteristic defect in the teachings of all our modern
seers—of all merely human seers of all the ages. They each in
his own way point out the defects and deficiencies of poor humanity, but with singular unanimity they fail to indicate definitely
anything like a precise course of action by which the alleged
failures of the centuries could be remedied. Ruskin is less open
to this charge than are many others of our modern prophets ; but
even he fails to solve the mystery of life so as in any way to
satisfy the restless yearnings of the human soul.

It will form an admirable series of exercises in composition to summarise the chief points in the extract, to write short original themes on some of the more important, and finally to reproduce one or two in the *style* (not necessarily in the language) of the author.

Sesame and Lilies.—This title, whether chosen for this purpose or not, aptly illustrates one of Ruskin's favorite ideas,—that *utility* should always be associated with *beauty*. *Sésame*, Gk. σησάμη, Arabic, *sim-sim*, is an Eastern leguminous plant, from the seeds of which a valuable oil is distilled ; while the beauty of the *lily* has been extolled from the days of Solomon.

The first of their lessons.—State concisely what are the three lessons of life specified. *First* — A. S. *fyrst*, superlative of *fore*. Derive *lesson*.

Mystery – μυστήριον, a secret rite, μυεῖν to initiate, μύειν = to close the eyes ; this word must not be confounded with *mystery*, or *mistery* a trade.

Who feel themselves wrong—who know also that they are right.—What is meant by a *paradox ?* Is this a paradox ? Give reasons for your answer.

Error.—Used in its strictly etymological sense = *wandering, straying*.

No rest—no fruition.—Why ? Derive and define *fruition*.

Love does but inflame the cloud of life, etc.—The metaphorical comparison of life to a cloud, or vapor, is a common one : and the lurid inflaming of this " cloud of life " is still more forcibly put further on in the extract (*see* p. 395, H. S. Reader) : " Our lives— not in the likeness of the cloud of heaven, but of the smoke of hell," etc. *See* also concluding paragraph, p. 396.

Industry worthily followed, gives peace.—With the general sentiment of this second lesson—that happiness and peace spring from earnest, honorable trial rather than from success—compare Dr. Arnold's " conviction that what he had to look for, both intellectually and morally, was not performance but promise," etc. *See* p. 350, Reader.

Into its toil.—What is the antecedent of *its ?*

Bequeathed their unaccomplished thoughts.—Note that it is not owing to the *accomplishment* of the thought, but to the earnest effort to " do it with their might" that these men " being dead, have yet spoken, by majesty " of the memory, and by the strength of the example they have *bequeathed*. A. S. *becwethan* = to affirm.

Six thousand years — according to Biblical chronology. Ruskin pays but little heed to the speculations of science.

Chief garden of Europe.—Anyone who has ever travelled through this romantic scenery must admit that our author exaggerates. No human power could ever render these Alpine crags the chief garden of Europe.

Noble Catholics of the Forest Cantons.—The Alpine region of Switzerland is almost entirely inhabited by Catholics, distributed through the following seven Catholic Cantons :—Lucerne, Zug, Schwyz, Uri, Unterwalden, Valais, and Ticino. In 1307, Uri, Unterwalden, and Schwyz (whence Switzerland) formed a confederacy against the House of Hapsburg, to which they had long been subject ; and in 1315, by the defeat of Leopold, Duke of Austria, in the memorable battle of Morgarten, these "noble Catholics" secured their independence, and thus laid the foundation of the Swiss Republic.

Noble Protestants of the Vaudois valleys.—These were the Waldenses, or followers of Peter Waldo, a merchant of Lyons, who began in 1180 to preach the doctrine of the sufficiency of the Scriptures. The sect suffered great persecution, especially in Piedmont, and were not finally granted full religious liberty till 1848, when the general upheaval of Europe forced Sardinia to allow them the same privileges as were enjoyed by their Catholic fellow-subjects. Since then the sect has spread widely ; but up till that time these "noble Protestants" were almost confined to the three valleys in the canton of Vaud, among the Cottian Alps, known as Lucerne, Perosa, and San Martino. (This last name must not be confounded with the little republic of San Marino, in Central Italy).

"Fevered idiotism."—This mental disease, known as 'cretinism,' is generally found associated with the physical malady, 'Goitre,' or swelled neck, by which the inhabitants of wholle valleys in the Alpine regions are afflicted. Though Ruskin so confidently asserts the disease to be due to the influence of undrained marshes, in reality very little is known as to its real nature, or its cause. It occurs also in some districts of the Andes and Himalayas, and is sometimes called *Derbyshire neck*, in consequence of its prevalence in that county of England.

The Garden of the Hesperides—in which the celebrated golden apples (oranges?) given by *Gé* (Earth) to *Hera* (Juno), on the occasion of her marriage to *Zeus* (Jupiter), were guarded by the four Hesperides (Ægle, Erythia, Hestia, and Arethusa), assisted by the dragon Ladon. One form of the myth located the garden north of Mount Caucasus; but the more popular account placed them, as in the text, west of Mount Atlas. Atlas assisted Hercules to slay the dragon and steal the apples, in requital for which service Hercules relieved his ally by sustaining the world for a day on his brawny shoulders.

An Arab woman—usually imitates the example of her great ancestress, Hagar, in devotion to her child ; so that such an incident as that which so well points Ruskin's moral must be a very rare exception.

Treasures of the East, &c.—This is rather in accordance with the old popular belief, long since exploded, than in harmony with the fact. *See* Macaulay's *Essay on Warren Hastings* for an account of the actual poverty of India.

Could not find a few grains of rice—The failure of the Indian Government to relieve the famine-stricken district of Orissa, in 1865, was due neither to apathy on the part of the Governor-General, Lord Lawrence, nor to the want of rice, of which there was abundance in other parts of India, but solely to the want of railroads and other suitable means of transport. The Indian Mutiny and this very famine in Orissa have stimulated the efforts of succeeding Administrations, and Hindustan is being rapidly covered with such a network of railroads as will make such a calamity well nigh impossible for the future. Is Ruskin correct in his estimate of the number who perished ?

Agriculture, the art of kings—from Cyrus down to "Farmer George."

Weaving ; the art of queens—as Omphalé, queen of Lydia, who taught her slave Hercules to handle the distaff, by beating that infatuated hero with her sandal ; Dejanira, wife of the same hero, punished him for a contemplated act of infidelity by sending him a tunic dipped in the blood of the centaur Nessus, a gift which caused his death and apotheosis ; the story of Penelope's web, woven and unwoven so constantly during her long faithful waiting for her lord, Ulysses,—and many other instances bear witness to the justice of the description in the text.

Their virgin goddess—was *Minerva* at Rome, *Athena* at Athens, where she was specially worshipped in her temple, the Parthenon, in which was a colossal statue of the goddess, executed by Phidias, the most renowned of Greek sculptors. She was known by various other names, and was worshipped as the patroness of all arts of men and women.

Word of their wisest king—Who ? and where does he thus write ?

Spindle—distaff—*Spindle* is the pin or stick from which the thread is *spun* ; the *distaff* = dise-staff, is the *staff*, or rod, which holds the *dise*, Low Dutch *diesse* = bundle of flax.

Tapestry—Gk. τάπης, Fr. *tapis* = carpet. Cf. "On the tapis."

Does not every winter's snow, &c.—Note the peculiar beauty of the rhythm ; and mark the characteristic directness of the appeal, with the terrible significance of the indictment "to witness against *you* hereafter, by the voice of *their* Christ," in whom *you* can have no part.

Lastly—take the art of Building, &c.—In this passage note the symmetry with which the long opening sentence is constructed. *See* last paragraph of Biographical Sketch. Give the derivation and meaning of :—*orderly, enduring, accumulative, unbalanced, prevalently,* "*civic pride,*" and "*sacred principle.*"

Men record their power—as in the pyramids and obelisks of Babylonia and Egypt : **Satisfy their enthusiasm**—as in the erection of columns to commemorate great victories. **Define and make dear**—Explain.

Worm of the sea—The coral insect, or *polypus*, is one of the lowest forms of animal life,—so low that it was classed as a plant by the early naturalists—hence they are fitly described here as "atoms of scarcely nascent life ;" but it is erroneous to speak of them as working,—"ramparts *built* by their labors "—for the polyps are absolutely passive in the matter, they do not build at all ; coral is simply the aggregation of the framework or skeletons of the insects, who must each die and rot away before its tiny skeleton can go to increase the bulk of the coral reef or rampart. **Rampart,** of which we have an older form *rampire*, is from French *remparer*, Lat. *reparare* = to repair, put in a state of defence.

Is it all a dream then ?—Note the rhetorical art with which the remainder of the extract is constructed, how skilfully he throws upon his readers the onus of replying to the grave questions raised, the stern rebuke to the realistic Positivism of the age, the adroitly contrived *dilemma* on either of whose horns objectors must inevitably be impaled, the almost imperceptible *climax* on which his argument rises, step by step, from questioning and uncertainty to decision and reality, till it closes with a trumpet call to arms, and we awake from the spell that has been upon us, glad to find that our *last* Dies Iræ has not yet written "its irrevocable verdict in the flame of its West."

MATTHEW ARNOLD.—1822-

RUGBY CHAPEL, NOVEMBER, 1857.—Extract XC., page 401.

Biographical Sketch.—So much has already been said in these pages about the great Rugby Public school, and the influence of its great headmaster, Dr. Arnold, that it seems superfluous to touch upon these subjects at all in treating, very briefly, of the life and works of his eldest and most gifted son.

MATTHEW ARNOLD was born in 1822, some six years before his father's removal from the rectory of Laleham to assume the head-mastership of Rugby. (*See* Biographical Sketch of Dr. Arnold, p. 32.) Dr. Arnold, with his firm conviction of the fundamental excellence of the great Public school system, the very essence of which is removal from purely home influence, sent his eldest son, at as early an age as possible, to the Public school of Winchester; and when the boy's character had thus been in some degree moulded, he returned to Rugby to complete his preparation for the University. Shortly after entering Baliol College, Oxford, he gained a scholarship; in the usual course he distinguished himself and his school, carrying off the Newdegate prize for English verse composition, and giving other evidences of sound scholarship, poetic taste, and critical acumen. In 1844 he took his B.A. degree with honors, and the following year was elected to a fellowship in Oriel college, another of the numerous colleges embraced within the same University. This position gave him, as it has given many others, a sufficient amount of learned leisure to prosecute his favorite studies; and to this period of meditative study we owe a good deal of what Matthew Arnold has done for literature.

In 1847 he was appointed private secretary by the late Lord Lansdowne, the most consistent politician, as Harriet Martineau describes him, of an age abounding in inconsistent politicians. During his connection with Lord Lansdowne, Arnold published his first volume of poems, anonymously, under the title of *The Strayed Reveller.* In 1851 the Lansdowne influence secured him the position of one of Her Majesty's Inspectors of Schools, a position in which he has been enabled to do almost as much for primary education in England as his father had accomplished for higher education; some of his Reports on the state of education on the continent of Europe being well worthy of consideration even on this more widely educated continent of America. His professional duties do not appear to have hindered his literary efforts; *Empedocles on Etna* appeared in 1853, and in the following year, 1854, a volume of poems first appeared with his name. Thenceforth the *name*, at least, of Matthew Arnold was known to

the outside world as that of a singularly gifted poet, the not unworthy
son, intellectually, of his distinguished father;—the *name*, for, in
sober truth, in little more than in name is he even now known to the
great mass of the light readers of our literature.   Nor is it likely
that his audience will ever be a large one—he does not write poetry
for the people, but for the scholarly few, who may be willing to
study the deeper, inner meaning of his allegorical themes, and
able to appreciate the severe classic simplicity of his style.   His
Merope, for instance, a tragedy modelled on ancient Greek forms,
while it can intensely delight the student in his library, and can
furnish him with endless food for thought and comparison, would
nevertheless be hissed off the boards of any theatre whose manager
might have the hardihood to venture on producing it.   This poem
was published in 1858, the year after he had been appointed to
the chair of poetry in the University of Oxford,—a position which
he ably filled for ten years, besides attending to his other somewhat numerous avocations.

His earlier prose works were produced during this period, consisting mainly of lectures delivered to his Oxford classes: *Lectures
on Translating Homer*, for which he advocated the employment of
the English dactylic hexameter, appeared in 1861; the *Essays
on Criticism*, in 1865; and lectures *On the Study of Celtic Literature*, in 1867.   All his prose works are critical, many of them
iconoclastic, some of them rather startling to the average orthodox
reader.   A fearless and outspoken critic, he has at least the rare
merit of having the courage of his opinions; nor does he now shrink,
apparently, from the idea of annihilation.   Of these disturbing
contributions to the sceptical literature of the age it is unnecessary
to say more than merely to mention their titles :—*Culture and
Anarchy, Literature and Dogma, God and the Bible*, and his numerous essays on similar topics have placed him in the foremost
rank of prose authors as far as style goes; but have been of little
value to the world of thought.   Any and every fool can suggest
doubts, difficulties, and dangers,—from Matthew Arnold more was
to be expected, but more has not been received.   He solves nothing, unravels nothing, makes nothing safe and sure.

RUGBY CHAPEL.

The mere catalogue of a man's writings gives no insight into
his real character, beyond the glimpse that it affords of his mental
bent as exhibited in the selection of his themes ; nor can any extract, however characteristic, do more than show what was the

prevailing tone of thought under which the extract was written. Hence it would be a serious error to conclude that in "Rugby Chapel" we have a portrait, a true likeness of the Matthew Arnold of to-day. The writer of the poem was a very different being in 1857 from the Matthew Arnold who appeared before his American audiences in 1883, and again in 1886, offering them the pressed, and dried, and dead flowers of 'Æsthetic Culture' as his only equivalent for the fruit of the Tree of Life, whose existence has become an unreal dream to him and the æsthetic school for ever and for ever. In 'Rugby Chapel' we feel the thrill of a strong human soul shaken by the doubts which must beset every mortal soul in its struggle to the light, but yet borne bravely up by the strong hope of reaching the goal at last, and this whirlwind state of unrest is, with almost terrific power, set forth in the dread allegories of the poem ; but in the writings and the lectures of his later years we find that this brave, struggling soul of his youth has at last attained to calmness and to rest—to the *calmness* of despair, to the *rest* of the grave of hope ! To hear Matthew Arnold on the platform, listlessly lisping forth platitudes about literature, dogma, culture, and so forth, one can hardly believe that there has ever been much of a struggle in the life of his calm, philosophic soul; but to read Rugby Chapel, and some others of his earlier short pieces, one must conclude that there must have been a period of mortal agony before such a nature could resign its birthright and heritage of immortality for the husks of unbelief.

The Autumn—evening.—Note the period of the year prefixed to the poem.

Silent.—Give the relation of this word. Mark the effect of chill, drear, loneliness, produced by these words and pictures in the opening stanza, and how fittingly they prelude the spiritual loneliness of the writer as depicted afterwards.

In whose bound Thou—art laid.—Where was Dr. Arnold buried? *See* Biographical Sketch, page 32.

By-gone autumns with thee.—Parse *with* fully.

Arosest.—How much more forcibly does this, the correct form, strike upon the ear, than the periphrasis 'didst arise !' cf. *upraisest, repressest, turnedst, beckonedst ;*—are these last two words more defensible on euphonic grounds than the others ? whether is the sibilation, in *arosest*, &c., a blemish or a beauty?

A call unforeseen, &c.—*See* Biographical Sketch of Dr. Arnold.

As under the boughs—as we might.—Parse each of the *as's. Bough*, A.S. *bóg* = an arm, the shoulder of an animal. Cf. *bow* of a ship.

Bare—unshaded—alone.—Note how persistently this horror of *loneliness* seems to haunt Arnold, not only throughout this poem, but elsewhere. E.g., in his short poem, *Isolation:*—

> " Yes ! in the sea of life enisled,
> With echoing straits between us thrown,
> Dotting the shoreless watery wild,
> We mortal millions live *alone*."

The same horror of loneliness may be met in **Clough,** and in not a few others of the same school of thought. It would seem, indeed, that each enquiring soul must pass through the stage of supposing that the road of conflict has never been travelled before, that *it* is the only soul now journeying over that lonely road so crowded by the multitudinous host of invisible spectres seeking for the truth, unknowing and unknown; that each must perforce imagine that it and none other has the dreary right to exclaim, with The Ancient Mariner:—

> "this soul hath been
> Alone on a wide, wide sea;
> So lonely 'twas, that God himself
> Scarce seemèd there to be."

By what shore tarriest thou now ?—An idea borrowed from the classical mythology, as far as the expression is concerned. But note the strong assurance of the writer that the " strong soul " is still at work in the " labor house vast of being." Force cannot die, though it ever tends to be dissipated; and hence " in some far-shining sphere, thou performest the word of the Spirit *in whom thou dost live*,"—not a very satisfactory, still less an orthodox view of immortality, but infinitely beyond the dreary Agnosticism of his later years.

Conscious or not.—Human philosophy cannot answer the much vexed question, " Shall we know each other there ? " And doctrinal hypothesis or discussion would be utterly out of place in these notes.

This was thy life.—A noble tribute to be paid to any man, even by a son, when fifteen years had enabled men to see clearly what had been the effect of the work and the life of the dead.

Achieving nothing.—With this, and with all this stanza, compare the sentiments expressed in the extract from Ruskin, " Of the mystery of life."

Midmost ocean—An imitation of the Latin idiom.

To be spent—to go round.—Show the relation and syntax of these phrases.

Eddy of purposeless dust.—Explain the meaning ; the use of the word 'effort' is not felicitous—no *effort* can possibly be *unmeaning ;* nor can it be *vain*, if we accept his father's higher standpoint, that what we have to look for is "not performance but promise."

Ah, yes! etc.—Analyze this period, ending at "devouring grave," and parse fully each word in it ; **dull oblivion,** cf. **Gray's** *Elegy:*—"dull forgetfulness."

Cheerful, with friends, etc.—The imagery of this magnificent passage is unequalled in any of Arnold's other works, is unsurpassed perhaps in our literature. The comparison of the arduous path of a would-be noble life to an Alpine ascent is familiar to all readers of LONGFELLOW's *Excelsior;* but it must be acknowledged that in vivid realism, in descriptive intenseness, and in the accumulation of awful accessories, Arnold has far transcended his American original. Regarding the passage merely as a descriptive account of an Alpine storm and its effects, we have to turn to BYRON's *Manfred* to find its parallel. It would be almost sacrilege to mar the beauty of such a passage by analyzing or dissecting it ; and it would be useless,—the poet is, in fact, so carried away by the vividness of his recollections of some grand lurid Alpine tempest, that he forgets to speak in allegory ; and so we have the commonplace ending of the catastrophe by the arrival at "the lonely inn 'mid the rocks" with its "gaunt and taciturn host," the reply to whose matter-of-fact question brings us back again to the original theme.

Woulds't not alone be saved.—The description of Dr. Arnold's unselfishness, and manly concealment of his own sorrows and heartaches exactly tallies with what we have learned of him from Dean Stanley, Tom Hughes (Tom Brown), and others of his pupils.

Who else—seem'd but a dream == who, but for the faith in goodness produced by example, would have seemed a mere dream, &c.

The race of men whom I see—is bad grammar; since the antecedent of *whom* is *men*, the article is required—*the* men. What would be the exact meaning of the words as they stand in the text ?

Unwillingly sees one—lost.—"It is not the will of your Father which is in heaven that one of these little ones should perish."—*Matt.* xviii, 14.

Marches the host of mankind.—The allegory is copied, not very closely, from the march of the Israelites into Canaan,—the spirits of "the noble and great who are gone" taking the places and discharging the functions, of Moses, Aaron, and Joshua. Note, in the closing stanza, how the special qualities of these great leaders are attributed to the departed "Servants of God."

Hour of need of your—race.—Parse the two *of's.*

GOLDWIN SMITH.—1823-

Biographical Sketch.—Few living writers of celebrity are so well known personally in Canada as GOLDWIN SMITH, and this fact, while it seems to render a biographical sketch unnecessary, in reality makes the task one of greater difficulty and delicacy than it would otherwise have been ; for it would seem ungracious to criticise the work and character of a distinguished guest with the same freedom that would be expected in dealing with a writer known to us only through his works, and to state bare biographical facts, without comment, would be at variance with the plan pursued hitherto in these NOTES.

He was born at Reading, in Berkshire, England, Aug. 13, 1823, his father being a physician in large practice, and consequently easy circumstances. On the completion of his school studies at Eton College (commemorated in Gray's celebrated and only natural ode), he entered Christ Church, Oxford, where he gained two scholarships and numerous other honors and prizes ; he graduated with first-class honors in classics, in 1845, and was shortly afterwards, 1847, elected a fellow and tutor of University College. In the year 1847 he was also called to the bar of Lincoln's Inn, but he has never entered on the practice of the law ; his legal studies, however, have been of great service as a mental discipline, developing the faculty of close investigation and reason so essential to the success of the historian. Shortly afterwards he was appointed assistant-secretary to the first, and was subsequently chosen as chief secretary to the second, Royal Commission appointed to enquire into the state of Oxford University ; his reports on these commissions are a valuable contribution to the literature of higher education, and gained their author his appointment as a member of the Education Commission, 1859. The year previously, 1858, he had entered on his duties as Regius Professor of Modern History in the University of Oxford, a position which he retained for eight years—resigning it then on account of the serious illness of his father. Some of his more important lectures to the students were afterwards published in book form as *Lectures on the Study of History*, 1861, and provoked the hostility of the *Westminster Review*, to whose adverse criticism the author replied in a series of trenchant letters in the London *Daily News*, subsequently collected and republished as *The Empire*, 1863. His *Irish History and Irish Character*, 1862, is an expansion of a lecture delivered on the subject before the Oxford Historical Society : It is animated by an obvious spirit of fair play, and a manifest desire to do jus-

H

tice by taking into consideration the causes of phenomena as well as their effects, the misfortunes of the people as well as their blunders and their crimes ; but it lies open to the one grave objection which may fairly be urged against all the historical theories of the author—they are all based on an estimate of human character derived from books, and not from actual contact with mankind. Another series of Oxford lectures, on the political history of England, was published in 1865, under the title of *Three English Statesmen,*—the three being Pym, Cromwell, and Pitt.

Besides attending to his professional duties and to the work of the Educational Committee, Goldwin Smith was, during this period, as he had been since his graduation, an active propagandist of advanced Liberal, or democratic, views, promoting them by purse, pen, and platform, and incurring thereby no small share of obloquy at the hands of his opponents. Readers of Lothair will recall the virulence with which the late Lord Beaconsfield, then Mr. Disraeli, assailed the "Oxford professor," and the petulance with which the professor replied to his assailant—an unworthy attack unworthily repulsed, the whole episode reflecting discredit alike on assailant and assailed. The cause of the Northern States was vigorously espoused by Goldwin Smith in a desultory series of letters to the London *Times,* and to his favorite organ, the *Daily News;* and among other instances of his Liberalism must not be forgotten the indiscreet zeal with which he flung himself and his money (the profits of *Three English Statesmen*) into the crusade got up by John Stuart Mill, and other visionary apostles of equal rights, against Governor Eyre, for the wholesome measures of timely severity by which he was enabled to nip the formidable Jamaica insurrection in the bud.

In 1868 he accepted the chair of English and Constitutional History in Cornell University, Ithaca, in the State of New York, his former sympathy and labors for the Union cause securing for him a most cordial welcome from all classes of the community. In 1871 he took up his residence in Toronto, Ont., where he has since resided. Ever since his arrival in Canada he has taken an active interest in the literary and political affairs of the country, his letters on political topics generally provoking a large amount of discussion, and sometimes (as in the Pacific Railway controversy sf some years since) contributing perceptibly towards the moulding of our institutions. Besides letters in the daily papers, he has been a regular contributor to the *Nation,* has conducted the *Bystander,* and has been the literary chief of *The Week.* Goldwin Smith is a clear and vigorous thinker, a singularly perspicuous and forcible writer, a fearless, if somewhat erratic, champion of the cause of civil and religious liberty.

MORALS AND CHARACTER IN THE EIGHTEENTH CENTURY.

The extract is taken from the author's life of Cowper, a monograph contribution to the "English Men of Letters" series. The style is so lucid that it will only need a few biographical notes to make the selection perfectly clear.

Cowper.—*William Cowper* was born in 1731, son of the Rev. John Cowper, rector of Great Berkhamstead, Hertfordshire, and nephew of Earl Cowper. He was educated at Westminster, where he suffered terribly from the "savagery at Public schools;" was admitted to the bar in the Middle Temple, 1754; was appointed clerk of the journals of the House of Lords, in 1763,—but was prevented, by extreme nervous diffidence, from deriving any advantage from these or any other appointment. Becoming insane from religious hysteria he was placed in charge of a physician, by whose skill he was sufficiently restored to reason, in 1765, to become an inmate of the family of the Rev. Dr. Unwin, of Huntingdon, to whose genial influence we owe the production of the *Task, John Gilpin*, and indeed most of his poetical effusions. As Goldwin Smith points out, to Cowper mainly we are indebted for the restoration of Nature to poetry. He died in the year 1800, having suffered during the last seven years of his life from occasional returns of his malady.

Spenser,—*Edmund*, author of our greatest allegorical *poem*, the *Faerie Queen* (1590-91), was born in 1553, d. 1599. **Shakspeare**—the greatest dramatist of all time, was born in 1564, at Stratford-on-Avon, in Warwickshire, England, where he died in 1616. **Milton**—the greatest of English epic writers, born 1608, d. 1674. These three are mentioned to heighten the contrast between poetry and *mere verse*. According to Goldwin Smith, Pope is not entitled to rank high among our *poets*, though he very justly awards him the praise of being an **arch-versifier,** i.e., not only a voluminous writer of verses, but an exceptionally skilful constructor of them. Most readers are, nevertheless, quite willing to accord to Pope a position as a poet only just below Dryden, while as a versifier he is far superior to him and all others of that age, if not of any age. Pope was born 1688, d. 1744.

Revolution of 1688—the Puritan Revolution.—Write notes on these two revolutions, their immediate and remote causes, and their consequences.

Nonconformists.—Explain the meaning or this word; also, of *Whig,* and of *Unitarian.*

Trulliber—Dr. Primrose.—*Trulliber* is one of the characters in **Fielding's** *Joseph Andrews*, where he is depicted as a course, sensuous, fat parson, intended as the type of the lazy, good-for-nothing parsons of the age. For **Dr. Primrose,** *see* notes on **Goldsmith's** *Vicar of Wakefield.*

Sinecurism and pluralities.—A *sinecure* is a living in which the holder has nothing to do but draw his salary; *pluralities* is the term applied to the holdings (rectories, incumbencies, &c.) held by a clergyman who holds more than one.

Hogarth,—*William,* 1697–1764, was one of the greatest satirical caricaturists the world has yet seen. His *Rake's Progress, Marriage à la mode,* and other series of cartoons on similar topics, give a vivid picture of the coarseness and licentiousness of the time.

Fielding and Smollett.—*Henry Fielding* (1707–1754), after a youth of wildness and dissipation, began, at the age of forty-two, to produce some of the finest fictions in the language. *Tom Jones, Amelia,* the *History of a Foundling,* and *Joseph Andrews* are his most important works. *Tobias George Smollett* (1721–1771), a Scotchman settled in London as editor of *The Briton,* in 1744. *Roderick Random, Peregrine Pickle,* and *Humphrey Clinker,* are his most important novels; he also wrote the continuation of Hume's History of England in a style not greatly inferior to that of his historical master.

Marriage à la mode.—*See* note on Hogarth, above.

Chesterfield—(1684–1773). The Earl of Chesterfield (Philip Dormer Stanhope) was one of the most brilliant, eloquent, witty, and wise noblemen of the age. He gained great *éclat* by his judicious administration as Lord Lieutenant of Ireland. His *Letters to his Son,* published the year after their author's death, are still quoted as final authority by compilers of manuals on etiquette; they show him to have been the heartless, soulless, courtly exquisite described in the text. He was, however, better than his age, which ought to go for something in the long account.

Wilkeses, Potters, and Sandwiches.—*John Wilkes* (1727–1797), the celebrated editor of the *North Briton,* and, by force of circumstances, the popular champion of the rights of liberty, was in private life one of the most profligate scoundrels that ever degraded and disgraced humanity; the notorious *Essay on Woman,* (a burlesque parody on Pope's celebrated *Essay on Man,*) composed by Wilkes and his boon companions, is couched in language that would not be tolerated in a brothel. *Lord Sandwich* held the office of Secretary of State in the Grenville Administration, and was, in profligacy at least, a worthy compeer of John Wilkes; in one respect, however, he enjoyed a proud pre-eminence in evil over his companion, for whereas the commoner, with all his vices, was at least an open and honorable political adversary, the peer disdained not to sully his noble rank and bring dishonor on his order by the blackest and most cowardly treachery—though he was the boon companion and *friend* (!) of John Wilkes, he was, at the time and all the time, employing paid spies to dog the steps of the great democrat, and was trying to procure evidence wherewith to hang his comrade by bribing a printer to furnish him with advance proof sheets of the *North Briton ! Noblesse oblige !*

Hell-fire Club.—The three clubs of this suggestive name in London were the culmination of the *Mohawk* clubs of Addison's era. George I. suppressed them in 1721 ; but it was not till the establishment of the regular police force to take the place of the old " watch" that the streets of London were rendered safe enough for the ordinary foot passenger at night.

Allworthy.—A benevolent and *all worthy* character in *Tom Jones.*

Sir Roger de Coverley.—The typical *country gentleman* of Addison's *Spectator.* See Sketch of Addison in Notes.

Westerns.—In Fielding's *History of a Foundling*, Squire Western plays an important part ; he is depicted as genial, jovial, irascible, ignorant, shrewd, but above all things as thoroughly selfish.

Positivists now promise—that the worship of *humanity* is to be the religion of the future ; at least that was the proposal of the founder of Positivism, the French philosopher, *Auguste Comte* (1798-1857), whose doctrines seem to be a combination of those of Fourier, St. Simon, and Hegel, i.e., a denial of the claims of theology and metaphysics, an abandonment of the search after the *causes* and *essences* of things, and a substitution, for these enquiries, of a search after natural *laws* by which to interpret natural phenomena.

Hogarth's Election—consisted of a series of four cartoon, caricatures of the incidents at an ordinary English election of the period.

Lady Huntingdon—was Selina, daughter of Earl Ferrers, and married to the Earl of Huntingdon, 1728. She was distinguished by her munificent charities, and stoutly befriended the early Methodist preachers, Wesley and Whitefield.

Stocks and the pillory.—The *stocks* was an instrument of punishment for petty offences, consisting of a strong wooden frame work with holes for inserting the feet, or hands, or both ; the *pillory* also consisted of a strong frame fastened to a pole, and having holes for the head and hands. Skeat gives up the etymology as obscure ; Webster merely gives Latin and Roman equivalents. May it not be from *speculatorium*, i.e., a spy-place, or place where the criminal is set up to be looked at? It is not from *pillar.*

Temple Bar --connected the Middle and Inner Temples, in the Inns of Court, in the building formerly occupied by the Knights Templar.

John Wesley—the founder of the Methodist Society, was born in 1703, and died in 1791 ; the course of the Methodist movement is too well known to need any comment.

Whitefield, *George*, 1714 1770, was one of the bravest and most hopeful of religious Reformers ; he was the best and most eloquent preacher of his day, and by the brilliancy of his elocution he often excited the envy even of Garrick and others scarcely less distinguished.

Johnson, *Samuel*, 1709 1784, was the literary king of the period : his biography, written by James Boswell, is one of the best works of the kind to be found in our own or any other language.

Howard, *John*, 1729 1790, the philanthropist and reformer of the prison system of England.

Wilberforce, William, 1759 1833, succeeded after years of agitation in carrying a bill for the Emancipation of the Slaves in all the British possessions in the West Indies.

THOMAS HENRY HUXLEY. —1825

A Liberal Education. *From* Lay Sermons, &c.—Extract XCIII., page 412.

Biographical Sketch.—Thomas Henry Huxley was born (1825) at Ealing, Middlesex, England, where, his father held the position of assistant teacher in the public school. Having acquired all the education the public school could give him, Huxley rapidly added to it such information as he could procure by himself, or with the help of his brother-in-law, a physician practising in Ealing. From 1842 to 1845 he continued the study of medicine and anatomy, already begun with his relative, in the Medical school at Charing Cross hospital. In 1846 he was appointed assistant-surgeon to H.M.S. *Victor*, at the Haslar hospital, in the neighborhood of Portsmouth ; and the following year he obtained the same appointment on board the *Rattlesnake*, then fitting out for a long cruise in the waters north and east of Australia During his five years' cruise Huxley was a constant correspondent of the Royal Society, in whose " Philosophical Transactions " many communications from his pen are embalmed; and so highly interesting and instructive were the facts communicated that he was made a Fellow of the Royal Society in 1851, and was awarded one of its medals. The materials collected during the voyage of discovery were afterwards published under the title of *The Oceanic Hydrozoa.* In 1854 he was appointed to the chair of Natural History in the Royal School of Mines, Jermyn street, London, where he has delivered many of his most brilliant lectures; and in the following year he was chosen Fullerian professor of Physiology at the Royal Institution. Since then he has been Hunterian professor of Comparative Anatomy and Physiology in the Royal College of Surgeons, and has acted as examiner in the London University. In 1870 he was chosen a member of the London School Board, where he histinguished himself by the fierceness of his opposition to the Roman Church, and to denominational education in the public schools. Though he is a great original thinker himself, he is better known in science as the interpreter of Darwin, and the propagandist of Darwin's doctrines. As a writer his style is singularly clear, concise, and accurate; it is, indeed, a thing to be wondered at that men so eminent in science as are Tyndall and Huxley should be at the same time such consummate masters of the art of expression. Either of them might be a great literary luminary, if he were not such a shining light in science.

A LIBERAL EDUCATION.

The extract is taken from one of Huxley's *Lay Sermons*, a series of scientific and semi-scientific lectures in the Jermyn street School of Mines to audiences composed principally of workmen. Note the plainness and directness of the language throughout, and the felicity with which even complicated thoughts are expressed. There is hardly a word in the whole extract that requires explanation.

Gambit—a special mode of opening a game of chess, Old Fr. *gamber*, to move, cf. Sanscrit *kamp* –-to move to and fro. Note how well the metaphor is sustained in the succeeding paragraphs.

Retzsch has depicted Satan—*Moritz Retzsch*, a German painter and engraver of great power and originality, was born at Dresden 1779, d. 1857 ; he was the great illustrator of the German poets. He depicted Satan in an original painting, of great though disputed merit, entitled THE CHESS-PLAYERS.

Playing for love—What is the force of this expression ?

Or, better still, an Eve—Why "better still ?"

Nature having no Test-Acts—to prevent students from entering the universal University, as the Test-Acts debarred them from the privilege of attending Oxford, Cambridge, and Dublin. What were the Test-Acts ? When and why were they passed ? When and why repealed ?

Take honors—the "Poll"—the plucked—the three classes into which candidates were divided as the result of the examination in the University. "*The Poll*" == the undistinguished crowd of mere *pass men*, A. S. *pól* == the head. Cf. the students' slang rendering οἱ πολλοί. The *plucked* == the rejected, said to be derived from an old University custom, whereby the proctor walked through the halls when the granting of a degree was under consideration, and whoever was of opinion that the degree should not be granted gently *plucked* the proctor's gown as he passed, in token, possibly, that the candidate should have his feathers *plucked*. Like most very old slang terms, its origin is doubtful.

Artificial education ought to be an anticipation of natural.—Huxley might have carried the province of artificial education a little further ; it ought not only to anticipate the natural education not yet received, but should also supplement by interpreting and adding to that already acquired.

That man, I think, etc.—This and the concluding paragraph would require a longer note than space will admit of. Try your hand at a critical estimate of Huxley's position, and do not be afraid to differ from him if you think his position untenable. No man would more delight in seeing such an exercise of a vigorous intellect than would the celebrated author of the extract.

ALGERNON CHARLES SWINBURNE.

THE FORSAKEN GARDEN.—Extract CI., page 422.

Biographical Sketch.—The "fleshly school" of sensual poetry is but lightly represented in our literature, and if it were entirely unrepresented neither the morals nor the literature of the community would greatly suffer by the omission. There is not the slightest fear of the morals of the English speaking world being permanently tainted by even the most musically composed descriptions of loves that are merely passions—passions that are merely lusts. The sober Briton recoils from the description of a Cleopatra that can find no image for herself and Antony so suitable as that of a wanton tigress yielding to the claws and fangs of her savage mate.

ALGERNON CHARLES SWINBURNE, son of Admiral Swinburne, and grandson of Lord Ashburnham, was born in London, 1837, educated at Eton, matriculated in Oxford, but did not remain to take a degree, making, instead, the tour of Italy in company with Walter Savage Landor. Whether from Landor or others, Swinburne early imbibed the agnostic dreariness of the age, and it is very probably due to the inevitable heart-coldness of all agnostic writings that the poems of the most gifted verse writer of our day are ignored by the great bulk of even the reading public. Many of his poems exhibit poetic faculties of the very highest order, combined with a mastery over the technical difficulties of metrical composition unsurpassed in any age ; but many of them are tainted by a materialistic sensuality, many by an agnostic negativeness,—qualities that have not yet been able to commend themselves to any large section of the community. *Atalanta in Calydon* was his first successful poem, his first volume of poetical effusions having fallen flat and unnoticed ; *Bothwell, Chastelard, and Mary Queen of Scots,* constitute a tragic trilogy, i.e., a series of three tragedies, each pivoting on the same central fact or idea as the others. His *Songs before Sunrise* is a poetic glorification of republicanism from an ideal standpoint. His *Songs and Ballads* provoked an unusual outburst of literary criticism ; and if the poet was somewhat roughly handled, he, of all men, has no right to complain, for no man more ruthlessly tramples on the most sacred beliefs of men, more scornfully scoffs at what most of us hold sacred than does Algernon Charles Swinburne.

THE FORSAKEN GARDEN.

This extract exhibits fairly some of the excellences of Swinburne, and some of his defects, though in a less degree. It illustrates his mastery of language and metre, betrays the pre-Raphaelite minuteness of his descriptive word - painting, shows his fondness for alliteration, and is sadly marred throughout by the shadow of agnostic uncertainty that has robbed so many of Mr. Swinburne's finest poems of their beauty and their strength. The metre is anapæstic, with occasional substitutions of equivalent feet, and here and there a redundant syllable. Scan the first stanza, marking the accented syllables. Is a trochee an equivalent for an anapæst? Give your reasons. Is an iambus? why? Is a spondee? why?

Ghost of a garden—Note the force of the expression : is it heightened by the alliteration? Point out other alliterations in the stanza. Is there a climax in the seventh line.

Long lone land – Note the persistency with which the poets of the sceptical school dwell on the idea of loneliness. *See* notes on Matthew Arnold.

The thorns he spares, &c.—After all, this Positivist way of looking at things is not much more cheerful than the old Christian way ; is it ?

Not a flower to be prest—Note the effect of the negatives here.

Burns sere—A. S. *seár* – to dry up.

Love was dead—is the modern 'utilitarian' way of stating these Gradgrind facts : with this contrast SOUTHEY in the *Curse of Kehama*,—

"'They sin who tell us Love can die.'"

The same dreary notion of annihilation pervades the next stanza.

Sheer cliff crumble—A. S. *scír* = bright, thence clear, unimpeded, perpendicular.

Death lies dead—the imagery in the last stanza is fine, and is quite in Swinburne's style. Is Death self-slain according to the views of orthodoxy ?

EDMUND WILLIAM GOSSE·—1849–

THE RETURN OF THE SWALLOWS.—Extract CV., page 437.

Biographical Sketch.—Among the minor poets of our day
EDMUND WILLIAM GOSSE is one from whom it is not unreasonable
to expect something greater and better than anything he has yet
achieved. Some of his *Madrigals, Songs, and Sonnets* exhibit not
only a refined and correct poetical taste, but also an unusual command over the difficulties of language and metre,—a command
without which poetical success is impossible in our hypercritical,
semi-poetic age. Gosse was born in London, England, in 1849,
his father being Philip Henry Gosse, a not undistinguished Fellow
of the Royal Society. Immediately after leaving school he was
appointed one of the assistant librarians at the British Museum,
and some eight years afterwards, translator to the Board of Trade.
He has several times visited the continent of Europe, not with the
listless apathy of a blasè sight-seer, but with the eager delight of
an enthusiastic student anxious to find out all that could be found
of the languages, the manners, and the literature of the people
with whom he came in contact. *King Eric: a Tragedy*, is the
principal poetic result of these visits, while in prose they have
given us his *Northern Studies*, a book worthy of a more cordial
welcome than it seems to have received at the hands of the reading
public. His *Life of Gray*, in the "English Men of Letters"
series, is his only other important prose work ; in poetry he has
written, in addition to the above, *On Viol and Flute*, a collection of
lyrical poems; *The Unknown Lover*, a drama, and another collection of fugitive pieces entitled *New Poems*, besides contributing
literary and critical essays to the Magazines and Reviews.

THE RETURN OF THE SWALLOWS.

This short poem requires very little in the way of comment or
annotation ; it has no moral to enforce, and is simply an unpretentious, though musical, description of an incident of ordinary
occurrence. The metre, dactyls and trochees, with occasional
substitutions, strikes the ear with a joyous ring well adapted to
the theme.

Shivering with sap—with the sap pulsating through it, as
the blood quivers in the veins of an animal.

Said the larks—This *said* is very tame.

Shoot—spirally—alluding to the spiral course of the British
lark in its rapid, almost vertical, ascent high into the air.

Fluted the thrushes.—The clear flute-like note of the thrush is more forcibly expressed here than is the clear note of the lark by the weak *said* of the second line.

White Algiers—with its bright bazaar "in the broad white dreamy square" would be the last halting place of the swallows before their northern flight. The city, like all Moorish towns, forms a conspicuous object in the landscape, the houses being all whitened to a dazzling brightness.

All at once—old sweet tones.—What is assonance ? Is this an example of it ? Explain your answer clearly.

Dingles—is a doublet of *dimbles*, which is only another form of *dimple*, the diminution of *dip*, i.e., a little hollow or dell.

Daffodils. —Other forms are *daffadilly*, and *daffadowndilly*, a flower of the lily tribe. The initial *d* is a corrupt addition to the word. Old Fr. *asphodile*; Lat. asphodelus ; Gr. ἀσφόδελος.

Alien birds.—Used in its original sense - strange, foreign.

The sad slave woman—gives a human interest to the poem and forms a touching picture of hopeless submission to her lot, as she looks up for a second from her ceaseless toil and sighs "to-morrow the swallows will northward fly " to that land of freedom that she, poor soul ! may never hope to reach.

FINIS.

www.ingramcontent.com/pod-product-compliance
Lightning Source LLC
Chambersburg PA
CBHW032011010726
47493CB00007B/2353